The Failure of the Occident.

THE FAILURE OF THE OCCIDENT

First edition. May 8, 2024.

ISBN: 979-8224078318

Written by Laurent Sueur.

Table of Contents

We are not at the beginning of the Ice Age, when a few Neanderthal tribes succeeded in protecting themselves from the cold in the south of Spain and survived, nor are we at the end of the Egyptian Old Kingdom, when drought led people to rebel against the regime and steal the food that enabled them to live a little longer, for we are faced with a situation which is more difficult... dangerous... desperate! Actually, the planet is overpopulated: eight billion people who hate one another threaten the survival of the human race. The next mass extinction may be that of mankind. Wars, pandemics, madness, barbarity, drought and famine are not new factors, but, this time, they are two problems which our forebears were not confronted with: abrupt climate change and the proliferation of nuclear weapons, both being able to put an end to man's adventure,

In times past, the Occident enlightened the world when confusion reigned; the crepuscular reason of some righteous nations used to restore order, but this lighthouse is diseased: it seems that it is unable to show societies the ways to reality and goodness. Unfortunately, if the Statue of Liberty drowns in the port of New York, there will be no future, for the rest of the world is not able to exert a civilizing influence on mankind.

But what does "Occident" mean? It is clear that many Muslims changed the meaning of this word and convinced people that it is almost a synonym for evil. Westerners are regarded as Crusaders who strive to impose their opinions and beliefs on the whole world. Hence, the Occident is a mysterious continent that stands between the underworld and hell, which is not a precise location! However, all Westerners know that this place exists and that historical factors determined this concept. In fact, it is the Romans who first individualized a territory where its inhabitants spoke Latin; in the east of the Roman Empire, people spoke Greek. Neither the habits nor religion determined this concept but the language. Hence, the Occident included Western Europe. The North and the lands located beyond the Rhine, where people did not speak Latin, were a mental frontier that protected the good, reason, grace and humanity from what was regarded as barbarity. Of course, as time passed, this linguistic entity was invaded by German tribes, but the Roman Catholic Church turned the uneducated pagans into polished Westerners who spoke Romance languages, said the prayers in Latin and behaved themselves. When Protestantism spread across Europe, the geography of the Occident did not change. Actually, it is the expansion of the British Empire that redesigned the Occident. North America, Australia and New Zealand became occidental territories; Westerners were more Protestant and republican than before; they were always white, but they did not only speak Romance languages: the Swedish, the Norwegians, the Dutch and the Danes were regarded as occidental people. As for the Germans, because of the spread of communism, their country enabled us to clarify the situation: West Germany was occidental because it was a democracy that favored capitalism, whereas East Germany was but an oriental communist dictatorship. This implies that the European countries that were communist countries and do not want to follow the rules of democracy and free trade do not belong to the occidental world. Hence, I would never dare to regard Poland, or Hungary, or the western part of Russia as occidental regions.

The aim of this book is thus to understand why that which was supposed to bring peace, civilization and goodness to the whole planet failed. The Westerners who lived during the 19th century thought that science would beget a better world, and it is a machine gun that murdered mankind in a trench in Verdun, which led Paul Valéry to say that he now knew that all civilizations were mortal, but the western societies that caused World War I cannot be regarded as civilization. Something is rotten in the West. The western nations that covered the whole planet with the shroud of sheer barbarity must not be regarded as civilization. Many things must be rotten in the Occident. The aim of mankind cannot be this hell, and it cannot end in this way. Why does man exist? Why does the universe exist? Man has not been created in order not to be humane or reasonable. Since these qualities exist, they must give birth to something different from this ordeal. Human nature let each individual become a human being or a monster. It is the individual who makes his or her own choice. Since social salvation depends on healthy social interactions, each individual is to take part in the wonderful adventure that will someday bring serenity to the human race. Someday, we will make the world a better place, and our happiness will enrapture the universe, which has not been created to witness our downfall.

Part I: The foundations of mediocracy.

Chapter 1: Some mistakes in education.

The aim of education is to enable people to understand human nature and the world in which they live so that they may interact with it and improve it. By means of science, teachers should teach their students how to discover the truth. Education is neither propaganda nor formalism, but it is clear that, in the Occident, it is often the first one, or the second one, or both at the same time.

A- A lot of subjectivity and very little science.

Any educational system perpetuates the beliefs that seemingly aim to enable society to survive. Whatever the culture, the language, the religion, the race, or the ideology of the students, teachers must make sure that they will not create antisocial monsters who will try to destroy society. All schools are Orwellian ministries of propaganda. The Chinese boy who submits to neo-communism corresponds to the Belgian girl who acknowledges the superiority of democracy. There is no morality here. Teaching must be based on the quality that characterizes mankind, namely humanity, for it is this quality that allows students to listen to people who do not share their opinions and discover the truth by means of science and research. For the time being, there is nothing but intolerance in all schools, including the occidental ones. Of course, some educational systems are less dysfunctional than others. Nonetheless, the best occidental schools are doomed to instill a sense of esprit de corps in students or indoctrinate them so that they may become conventional ordinary people who will never question the system

The worst educational system is that of France. It was established in 1881, when the republican government decided that education would be free and compulsory. Hence, hordes of republican primary school teachers brainwashed generations of pupils because it was the most efficient way to lead future citizens to believe that the republican regime was the best regime ever. For this reason, ethics classes were important elements of this propaganda scheme, but history classes were even more important. Thanks to republican history, teachers propagated the hatred of Germans, who were accused of having stolen Alsace and Lorraine: French territories where people spoke German. The "Jerries" became the arch-enemies of the French, all the more so because their regime was regarded as a kind of dictatorship. This propaganda was very efficient: in 1914, the young Frenchmen who went off to war were firmly convinced that Germany had to be destroyed.

After World War II, propaganda at school changed natures. Since most teachers were communists, they distorted reality and inspired anti-Americanism among their students, which still exists. Today, French students continue to learn at school that it is the French soldiers who liberated the French from the Nazis, whereas the Americans, the bad guys, nuked the poor Japanese civilians.

Even in universities, objectivity is not that common. It seems less serious because students are older: they are supposed to be able to easily distinguish truth form lie. However, when people undergo years of propaganda, they are not able to acknowledge the truth anymore. Moreover, scientists, I mean the persons who study exact sciences, are not more objective than literature or history professors.

In the United States, the tobacco industry, for instance, has been spreading disinformation for years in order to conceal the dangers of smoking. With regard to secondhand smoke linked with heart disease (1), the first epidemiological studies were published in the mid-1980's, which led the tobacco industry to recruit physicians and scientists, at the end of the 1980's, to minimize the importance of this factor. Since, in the USA, universities need patrons to function, collusion between private interests and higher education is facilitated. Scientific journals, which should be independent in order to guarantee their objectivity, are sometimes financed by the tobacco industry. Hence, the papers are carefully examined, and those which emphasize that smoking is dangerous are not published (2). Those that are published systematically underestimate the dangers of smoking. For example, from January 2013 to June 2015, almost all the authors who published a paper about tobacco or nicotine in *Regulatory toxicology and pharmacology* (3) had ties to the industry, and 76% of those papers drew conclusions that were positive for the tobacco industry; no paper drew negative conclusions. However, social pressure can improve the situation. Nowadays, the editors of scientific journals are cautious about publishing research by authors who are linked to this industry (4).

That being said, the one subject that enables observers to measure the objectivity of an educational system is history, for it is the most efficient means to manipulate the masses and invent social myths that strengthen the sense of belonging.

In the USA, in middle schools and high schools, although one cannot say there is a lot of propaganda, the students' textbooks give sometimes a distorted view of the past. In fact, the past is far too present! I mean that there are lots of anachronisms. Even young students can understand that the people of the past did not think or behave like them; so teachers should not transpose present situations or worries to the past (5). For instance, the authors of *Glencoe world history* (6) keep asking students to connect the past to the present picturing themselves as Babylonian rulers, ancient Greece citizens, and medieval students and merchants, which they will never be! This forbids them to develop their capacity for abstract thinking.

Fortunately, some teachers who are more intelligent than others are neither deceived by the system nor influenced by what it produces: free will exists, but it is impossible to know whether those free electrons have a major influence or not. However, the goodwill of some professors gave birth to a very good textbook (7) aimed at helping college students to improve their level. It is simple; the sources are easy to find; the inglorious moments of American history are not concealed; women are not forgotten. Hence, in a system that is quite subjective, some people try to fight against ignorance.

B- To perpetuate the past.

In the Occident, the educational systems are profoundly inequitable. In fact, most of the time, private schools coexist with public ones, which allows the wealthiest parents to send their children to the "best" boarding schools. They thus befriend people with the same social background, which keeps them in a homogeneous social milieu that turns them into conservative individuals. Even the psychopathic offspring of the ruling class end up sharing the same conservative views. Of course, there are always scholarship students who, like Boris Johnson at Eton College, do not belong to the bourgeoisie that rules the country, but years of acculturation can transform any proletarian into a credible conservative individual. The past keeps on existing in this fashion; so do social illusions. Besides, in democracies, boarding schools are the first level of activism. There the students begin to build relationships and therefore a proto-political network that is also a professional network. At the university, they keep on behaving in the same way: enslaved by their beliefs, they perpetuate tradition, and endogamy reinforces this process.

The French educational system is quite unfair, all the more so because inequity is institutionalized. Public schools coexist with private ones which are not that private because they are supervised by the government. In fact, it is the state that pays the salaries of the teachers, shapes the curriculum and grants the diplomas to the students. The fees are reasonable, but all parents cannot afford to pay them. Besides, principals do not allow bad students to register. This is illegal, but, because of the collapse of the public school system, they are so many students who want to register that they can easily circumvent the law. They also keep threatening to expel them if their marks are not good, which compels them to take lots of private lessons. In grade 11, in neighborhoods where demand for such services is high, all the students are good and obedient.

In the public school system, there are also high schools where there are classes that are better than others. Thanks to options (Chinese, Russian, math for advanced students...), the principal forms groups that include good pupils and the children of the teachers who work there. The teachers whom he likes are allowed to teach those students their subjects, whereas the others are in charge of the worst groups. The children who are expelled from private and public schools end up in establishments that are financed by the customers and where the fees are high. Since these pupils are misfits, in spite of lots of lessons, they don't always pass the exams or fit in.

Inequality worsens at college level. The people who attended the "best" high schools are able to pass the competitive exams that will enable them to study in the best universities (École Polytechnique, École Normale Supérieure...), where they will start building a professional and political network which will enable them to get a good job and belong or continue to belong to the upper middle class. Those who cannot will attend an ordinary university, where they will often study subjects that will not help them to find employment. As for those whom the French sociologists call "the heirs", they will attend a business school, where they will learn techniques that will enable them to manage their parents' business.

Parliaments mirror this social inequality, and the congresspersons who belong to the Democratic Party are as conservative as the Conservatives. Most of the time, they are apparatchiks who attended the same schools, studied the same subjects, belong to the same social class and do not really want to change the system.

In the United Kingdom, many members of the parliament attended boarding schools (8). Among those who were elected in 2019, 44% of the Conservatives, 33% of the Liberal Democrats and 19% of the Labour MP's had attended boarding schools. 87% of the MP's had received a degree and 20% had gone to the universities of Oxford or Cambridge, which shows that this political milieu is quite homogeneous. In fact, it has never been that homogeneous, for, since 1979, the cultural and social disparities between the members of the major political parties have been diminishing. For instance, in 1979, 49% of the Conservative MP's, 27% of the Liberal Democrat MP's and 21% of the Labour MP's attended the universities of Oxford or Cambridge. In 2019, 29% of the Conservative MP's, 28% of the Liberal Democrat MP's and 21% of the Labour MP's went to these universities. This piece of information parallels the socio-professional background of the MP's. Although we don't know what were their occupations before the general elections, official statistics show that the candidates who ran in the 2015 general election belonged to the same social class: the middle class. There were very few manual workers (3%) and farmers (1,1%) and no wealthy people.

In the USA (9), 96% of the congresspersons and senators went to the university and received a degree. Unfortunately, we do not know whether they attended certain ones. Before the 2020 election, 44% of them were state or territorial legislators, 21% teachers, and 14,5 % congressional staffers, which means that those people were well acquainted with the "public service" and that they did not mirror the American society at all.

In fact, in both democratic systems the same middle-class members with a petit bourgeois mentality rule both countries. The wealthy and the poor are absent. This milieu is so homogeneous that there cannot be major changes, for either the Conservatives or the Democrats want to save the regime that enabled them to come to power. The poor and the rich are outcasts who would like to choose their future and that of society. When they cannot, both groups usually rebel.

C- To assess the damage.

We can now assess the damage caused to the youth and society thanks to international studies that evaluate the knowledge of students in language, math and sciences. Each time the TIMSS and PISA (10) reports are published, western governments tremble with fear and citizens pity themselves, all the more so because Asians get better marks than the other nations, which puzzles the Occident, for it is not that easy to understand why the countries that made the world what it is are mediocre.

However, statistics must not deceive us. For instance, in the Pisa report, the Chinese communist government authorized only the publication of the statistics for Beijing, Shanghai, Jiangsu and Zhejiang, which are either large cities or urbanized regions where the authorities and parents invested more money in education than in rural areas. Macao and Hong Kong, two special territories of Communist China, are also cities; so is Singapore, which is an independent country. In fact, when Asian regions are less urbanized, like Chinese Taipei (Formosa or Taiwan), the students' exam results are less brilliant. That being said, Asians in general take education seriously. In Los Angeles (in Southern California), for example, during the COVID-19 pandemic, when school were rarely open, Asian parents succeeded in teaching their young children English, and their reading skills improved, whereas those of the whites, Black Americans and Latinos diminished. We notice that some Asians, even when they don't live in Asian countries, share the same opinion on knowledge.

As to linguistic abilities, it is clear that some languages are harder to learn than others. For instance, children strive hard to learn Chinese because there is no alphabet: each ideogram must be learned by heart. Russian and German are inflected languages that compel students to master grammar. It is not easy to learn English because there are many words, lots of weird rules and some regional differences. On the other hand, French is a simple language, for there is a limited number of words and, nowadays, people do not use all the tenses: they almost always use a kind of timeless present. Besides, for various reasons, in many countries, at home, students do not speak the language in which there are taught the different subjects, which does not facilitate learning. Hence, in order to estimate the linguistic abilities of students, we must take those two factors into consideration.

In the 2019 Pisa study, the best pupils were from Beijing, Shanghai, Jiangsu and Zhejiang, which is not surprising, since almost all of them (99,5%) speak Chinese at home. Hence, parents could help them when they encountered difficulties. The pupils from Macao and Hong Kong were good too, but in these territories, 19% of them do not speak Chinese at home, which shows that the educational system of the two cities is quite efficient. As for the students from Chinese Taipei, where 16% of them speak other languages at home, they are not as good as the ones from Macao and Hong Kong, which might be due to a lower rate of urbanization.

In the USA and the UK, in 2019, students scored almost the same number of points although there are more students who do not speak English at home in the US (17%) than in the UK (12%), which shows that the American educational system is more efficient than the British one. This fact was confirmed, in 2022, by the drop in the British students' performance. As for the exam results of the French pupils, they are much lower than those of the Americans and British, which is surprising since the language is much simpler and there are only 11% of the students who do not speak French at home.

However, the scores in math are more meaningful, for this subject relates to logic. In fact, it enables observers to measure the intelligence of pupils and people.

Once again, the Chinese are much better than the others, but the British and the Americans' marks were higher in 2019 than in the previous reports (12), and they hardly dropped in 2022. The Americans can even pride themselves on having enabled girls to be as good as the boys, which is very rare in the world since societies, customs and males keep telling them that there are subjects and jobs reserved for boys and those that are reserved for girls. Of course, in 2019, there were lots of very good pupils (51%) in the Singaporean math classes, but the Americans and British were doing well since 14% of the American students and 11% of the British ones excelled in math; the median was 5%.

As for the French students, their marks are getting lower (13). There are only 2% of very good math students. In fact, now the French students are as mediocre as those from New Zealand and Romania. From 1995 to 2019, they have experienced a drop of 46 points in math, which means that a 13-year-old French pupil of the year 2019 has the same level of knowledge as a 12-year-old French pupil of the year 1995. The 2022 Pisa study shows that this process is accelerating, which proves that the French educational system is collapsing.

D- To solve the problem.

Westerners are well aware of the limits of the educational systems. They question the teachers' knowledge and objectivity and wonder whether children will learn anything in places that can be disorderly. The COVID-19 pandemic worsened the situation. Schools were closed for a long period of time; children had to stay at home; all parents had to homeschool them. Some teachers were able to send documents to their students and mark their exercises, others taught classes online, but most parents were alone and bemused. Thanks to vaccination, all the children went back to school in 2022. In the USA, tests (14) show that very few students were able to make progress. Disadvantaged children struggled to learn because their parents were not knowledgeable enough to explain what they themselves did not really understand. Hence, as usual, African Americans and Latinos' academic skills diminished. Actually, the only parents who could handle this strange situation were those who were used to educating their children at home.

In Europe, homeschooling has always existed. It was a type of education which the wealthy favored. Kings like Louis XVI, Louis XVIII and Charles X (who were brothers) were educated by tutors who were clergymen. The aristocracy did the same: they hired a priest who taught their children the basics of reading, writing and arithmetic. Then boys attended an exclusive college where teachers were clergymen. Princes did not. Louis Philippe d'Orléans was the first and last king of France to send his eldest son, at the beginning of the 19th century, to this kind of establishment, for he believed that a man whose destiny was to rule the country had to know its inhabitants or at least the elite.

There was also another type of education which enabled the pupils who could not attend a school to be educated: distance learning. The Australians (15), were the first to systematize primary education by correspondence. In the 1920's, the Australian states allowed the children who lived three or four (South Australia) miles from the nearest school to work in this way. They did not charge fees for tuition; some of them paid the postage both ways and provided textbooks. Hence, the young pupils received leaflets and had to send their exercises to a school, where primary school teachers marked them. The state supervised those children even though their parents were the real teachers. Most of the time, it was the mothers who, reading aloud what was written in the leaflet, taught their children to read and write. This was a kind of homeschooling supervised by the state, which still exists. However, what is taught is designed by the state; those children learn what all the children learn at school. So, if there are mistakes in a course, all pupils learn them and perpetuate falsehood.

In fact, homeschooling that is not connected to any kind of institution is the only counter-measure. In this case, parents choose what their children learn, and most of the occidental governments monitor students' progress. It is clear that if the educational systems worked, parents would not bother to educate their children in this way.

Although there are no statistics on the reasons why some American parents choose to homeschool their children (16), when they give their opinions, observers understand that American schools and high schools are not always the best place where one can learn, since they sometimes enable people who neither demonstrate the same level of proficiency in most subjects nor want to achieve the same objective to group together. Besides, the scientific purpose of those institutions is not obvious. There are so many useless cultural interactions that one wonders whether students learn sciences or how to become conventional American citizens. A school is not a place where civil servants homogenize culture or demeanor. A school where teachers neither promote true science nor track students accurately is not a school anymore. No wonder these parents attribute their choice to poor academic performance, violence, racism and bad influence.

In 2022, the Britons published statistics (17) which show that parents chose to homeschool their children because of the COVID-19 pandemic (19%) and for reasons linked to their philosophical believes or life style (19%) and to physical or psychological problems(18%). 12% of them were dissatisfied with the educational system. Very few parents (1%) stated that their children had been bullied. Since very few British pupils are homeschooled, one must conclude that the Britons do not question their educational system, although it is inequitable. In fact, for the time being, in the Occident, most people are like sheep.

The most intelligent ones form their own opinions once they are adults, but how can you form your own opinions when you have learned falsehoods for years and years? Can a child who is used to accepting many statements as valid disentangle the myth from reality once he or she is an adult?

Chapter 2: When democracies lie.

What is the function of lies? Children's lies are aimed at concealing a misdemeanor in order not to be punished by people who are supposed to tell them what good and evil are and to compel them to submit to fairness. Their lies are also aimed at manipulating adults so that they may satisfy a desire. However, politicians are not children, and if they behave like them, one must acknowledge that they are immature people who should not have been elected: politics is not a children's game. At last, some lies are not lies anymore. In fact, reasonable people regard them as lies, although they are ideas and actions that reveal a misunderstanding of reality.

Any regime should be based on truth, for it is the only way to understand problems and solve them. Any regime that lies is doomed to failure. Unfortunately, it seems that lying is a widely shared political habit, which is becoming a major component of occidental democracies. It is clear that democracy compels politicians to entice citizens to make a choice between people who, most of the time, cannot demonstrate that they are the best candidate, since they have not held the office they are running for. Once they are elected, they continue putting a gloss on what they do in order to be re-elected. However, some lies are bigger than others, and some political shenanigans have more serious consequences than others.

A- A war in Iraq.

After the attacks perpetrated on the 11th of September 2001, which showed the weakness of the so-called world's cop, the American government put the blame on Islamism. Westerners' everlasting hatred of Islam was kindled by the people who dropped along the endless silvery windowpanes of the blazing World Trade Center, which then collapsed, covering Manhattan with debris and plunging the Occident into consternation. George Bush, the Protestant, bemused American president, soon defined an axis of evil, which took us back to the Middle Ages. Once again, we were Crusaders, and the Muslims were the wicked ones who covered the world in blood.

We are not in the heads of the politicians who are supposed to maintain world order, but if we were, we would certainly be appalled by their lack of intelligence and knowledge. However, after these terrorist attacks, the Americans strove hard to find the culprits. Saddam Hussein was a credible suspect: he was a kind of dictator and Westerners had given him lots of chemical weapons during the Iran-Iraq war. Osama bin Laden, who had allegedly financed the 9/11 attacks, might have taken refuge in Iraq. It was easy for Tony Blair to make a man who desperately wanted to find culprits, G. W. Bush, believe that Saddam was on the Occident's hit list.

It is clear that the British prime minister was shocked by the attacks. On the 12th of September 2001 (1), he writes a letter to the American president, which shows that he thinks that this is just the beginning of something bigger. He believes that those terrorists can get hold of biological or chemical weapons since there are some governments and individuals who trade in weapons of mass destruction. He does not say that he suspects that the Iraqi government is one of them. It is only on the 11th of October 2001 that he mentions this country, in a letter to G. Bush in which he tells him that it is high time they devised a strategy aimed at getting rid of Saddam Hussein. This means that, at that date, although he has not identified the culprits, he wants to prevent the people who have designed what he believes to be a plot to destabilize the Occident to get the weapons that will enable them to do so. He is already convinced that the end justifies the means.

However, it is his note on Iraq, dated 28 July 2002, that reveals the manner in which he will manipulate the American president and the

European nations, especially those that are reluctant to go to war (the Germans and the French). The core of Blair's machinations consists in provoking Saddam Hussein into refusing the UN inspections, which will show that he has something to hide. Then the British officials make up stories about his weapons of mass destruction, his links with Al Qaeda, the terrorist organization, and his attempt to secure nuclear capability. They also emphasize that the regime is brutal and inhumane in order to entice the representatives of the democratic nations to the United Nations to back the invasion of Iraq. Although Blair is firmly convinced that Saddam possesses chemical weapons, he invents the rest. He keeps saying that he wants to spread the values of freedom, democracy and tolerance, but he does not care about the soldiers who will die during the forthcoming war.

As predicted and planned by the British prime minister, the Iraqis did not really co-operate with the UN and the IAEA inspectors, which legitimized the invasion of Iraq.

However, Tony Blair's lies were so clumsy that they did not really deceive intelligent people. On the 5th of February 2003, when Colin Powell, secretary of state, peruses the speech almost dictated by the British, which he will have to deliver, he is utterly appalled. When the television networks broadcast his speech and the pitiful so-called pieces of evidence showing bunkers and chemical weapons production facilities, most viewers snigger. On the 8th of February 2003, Blair's machinations are disclosed by the newspapers, but the Bush administration confesses that they were no weapons of mass destruction in Iraq only in 2005.

As for the Britons, they set up a commission to investigate the British government's shenanigans. On the 27th of November 2009, William Ehrman, a high-ranking official who worked for the Foreign Office from 2000 to 2002, declared that the prime minister knew that there were no more weapons of mass destruction in Iraq when he sent the British troops to that country. When Tony Blair was interrogated by John Chilcot, the chair of the Iraqi Inquiry, he stated that on the eve of the invasion (2) he had asked the chair of the Joint Intelligence Committee to confirm that Saddam Hussein had weapons of mass destruction; he had answered that he had.

Several years later, on the 6th of July 2017, Laura Kuenssberg interviewed John Chilcot, and she kept on asking him whether Tony Blair had told the truth during the inquiry, which embarrassed him. He tried to excuse him by saying that the politician was under very great emotional pressure during those sessions; then he confessed that the ex-prime minister had not been as honest as he should have been. Tony Blair appeared to be a manipulative liar who had imposed his opinions on the American president and on many EU members, which had led to a war and destabilized a region which did not need that. Some people had died during that war, especially 179 Britons. This time it was not a ruthless dictatorship that had caused a war, but an occidental democracy.

B- The Brexit.

The relationship between England and the "Continent" has always been bad for historical reasons. Actually, if England had not had so many ties to France during the Middle Ages, there would not have been so many wars between both countries. Hence, when six European countries signed the treaty of Paris, in 1951, establishing the European Coal and Steal Community, the British regarded it as another French eccentricity. As time passed, the economic advantages moved them to enter the European Economic Community, and they most certainly benefited from the "free market". They did not even complain when their most faithful enemies, namely the French, became the owners of so many English bakeries and restaurants, turning London into a French city!

In fact, the big mistake was that of the Labour government, when, in 2004, it decided to implement immediate open borders with the ten states that had just joined the European Union (3). Most of them were Eastern European countries. The members of the government thought that the number of immigrants would be small (between 5 000 and 13 000 people per year), but each year around 127 000 workers born in those countries settled down in the United Kingdom. Although the British economy was quite dynamic, those low-skilled workers (4) competed with the British ones for employment, and there was a certain pressure on wages for low-skilled British workers. We don't know whether it was a culture shock, but we now know that it was a social time bomb.

In 1975, 67% of the voters had agreed to join the EEC (5). 38% of the Britons thought that there were not too many immigrants in the UK, and 26% had declared that there were too many of them. In 2015, 11% of the Britons stated that there were not too many immigrants in the UK, whereas 51% said that there were too many. The mass migration of Eastern Europeans to the UK had moved the working class to reject the system which impoverished them. The people who lived in districts where there were lots of low-skilled workers (6), Eastern European immigrants and much pressure on the public health system voted to leave the EU in the referendum, whereas the middle classes voted to remain in the EU. Actually, the social turmoil enabled unscrupulous politicians to manipulate the masses.

It is hard to evaluate the influence exerted by Boris Johnson over people who were already convinced that the UK had to leave the European Union. However, his actions during the Brexit campaign show that disinformation played a key role in it.

In 2016, he was mayor of London and a member of the British parliament and of the Conservative Party. Although the leader of his party, Prime Minister David Cameron, campaigned to convince the voters that remaining in the EU was advantageous to Britons, he chose to hold the pro-leave side of the Brexit debate (7). It is a strange demeanor, for the members of a same political party share the same opinions, or else they change parties and become opponents. Boris Johnson is so immature and weird that one must examine the long-running rivalry between him and David Cameron. In spite of a facade of close friendship with him, the envious Boris Johnson coveted his job, the best job in the world. The petit bourgeois adolescent who made his mates laugh at Eaton College, in order to be popular, to be loved, and to feel as if he belonged to the elite, wanted to become the leader of the pack. He was maneuvering the public into enabling him to get the best job in the world, and the end justified the means.

Hence, he buttered voters up by saying that if the UK left the EU, the British government would recover 350 million pounds sterling each week, which would be available for extra public spending. On the 17th of September 2017 (8), David Norgrove, chair of the UK statistics authority sent a letter to Boris Johnson in which he told him that he had mistaken gross for net contributions, which was dishonest and clear misuse of official statistics. The then Foreign Secretary did not change his mind. Actually, his perception of reality is poor, which is why we cannot regard him as an ordinary liar. He is the kind of person who believes that the truth is a matter of interpretation. He is not a reasonable scientist who examines facts and then draws conclusions from objective manifestations. The eccentric ex-mayor of London has been behaving in a strange way since his childhood. Journalists keep drawing the public attention to his misdemeanors, but they do not question the system that enabled citizens to vote for an old child who always says that he has done nothing wrong, although he has been caught in the act of refurbishing his flat with the taxpayer's money, attending parties during a lockdown, and so on.

Furthermore, propaganda and lies are now spread by means of communication which increase their efficiency and exacerbate unreality. The so-called social media were invented in order to enable people to communicate with people whom they rarely know and will almost never meet. If they were intended to enable them to share accurate information, they failed miserably. Social media are a kind of amplifier that moves wolves to yell louder. Users are almost convinced that they are personages who are to inform their worshipers of the minutest details of their insignificant lives. Everybody becomes what democracies forbid them to be: omnipotent idols. Ordinary lives become extraordinary; ordinary people turn into psychotic dictators. This primal narcissism prevents them from perceiving reality as it is. Social media are a kind of barrier between individuals and the outside world.

Hence, it is little wonder that some people tried to influence voters by means of social media during the Brexit campaign. Unlike official media, which are compelled to check the information and enable each candidate to present his or her manifesto, they were a kind of Far West where manipulators spread rumors and false information. Some scientists collected tweets (short messages sent on Twitter) on the topic of the UK/EU referendum (9). In their dataset, they had 3485 tweets from 419 troll accounts (accounts belonging to "online manipulators"), which were collected between the 29th of August 2015 and the 3rd of October 2017. Those tweets were about the Brexit referendum and topics that were expected to influence the vote (refugees and immigrants for instance). The largest number of troll tweets was collected on the day of the referendum (the 23rd of June 2016), and most of them were in favor of leaving the EU.

This partial study does not prove that, on that day, voters were greatly influenced by the propaganda they read on their mobile phones, but it shows that western democracies are slipping into a twilight zone between crowd manipulation and delusion.

C- The Trump experiment.

In November 2016, the Americans elected a compulsive liar as their president, which must lead us to question the American citizens' capacity for distinguishing truth from falsehood and for choosing a person who will be able to fulfill his or her duties. Donald Trump was a boastful billionaire who was famous for his television show (The Apprentice) and his overstatements. No wonder he continued to take liberties with the truth once he was elected.

However, during his presidency, his idiosyncrasies worsened. Actually, he made 30 573 false or misleading claims (10). He averaged six false or misleading claims a day in his first year as US president, sixteen in his second year, and thirty in his final year. There was a spike in the number of claims about immigration in November 2018, during the midterm elections, in order to convince voters to continue supporting his immigration policies. In October 2020, as he was recovering from COVID-19, he kept sending pseudo-scientific messages about this disease: that month, the claims amounted to nearly four thousand!

So that he might reach a wide audience, Donald Trump would use his Twitter account (11). During his presidency, he sent more than 25 000 messages (which included tweets and retweets); it makes an average of eighteen tweets per day. From the middle of the year 2019 to the end of the year 2020, the number of tweets and retweets increased significantly.

Thanks to Twitter, on the 19th of December 2020, at 1:42 am, the US president could send this message to his followers (12): "Statistically impossible to have lost the 2022 election. Big protest in D. C. on January 6th. Be there, will be wild." Did he really believe that he had not lost the election? Figures are scientific evidence: one cannot question election results when official observers declare that there were no irregularities. Trump is so insincere that we must regard this tweet as a story he consciously made up in order to kindle the wrath of his supporters, which proved to be efficient.

In fact, an anonymous employee (12) told the committee that investigated the attack on the Capitol that he saw a rise in violent rhetoric online following that tweet, and many people who were interrogated by the committee declared that they had resolved to go to Washington DC (some of them carrying weapons) after they had read it.

On the 6th of January 2012, at a "Save America" rally, Donald Trump repeated that there had been election irregularities and suggested to his supporters that they take action to protect their country. Many of them headed for the Capitol as congress was beginning the electoral vote count which would determine the winner of the presidential election. Some rioters entered the building. Confusion reigned. Western Europeans were appalled, all the more so because most of them despised the man whom they regarded as a jester. Finally, the ex-president, in a Twitter video, told the insurgents to go home in peace.

Was it an attempted coup d'état? Some people said that it was (14) because participants included members of right-wing militias, terrorist groups, neo-Nazi and white supremacist organizations, and conspiracy groups. They emphasized that, in the past, President Trump had shown that he had some sympathy with the far right ideals. However, Donald Trump is not Hitler, and those militias do not resemble the Waffen-SS. A coup d'état is a well-organized action characterized by armed people who methodically take control of the army, the police and the government. The attack on the Capitol was just a demonstration that aimed to intimidate the congresspersons. Did the rioters expect them to vote again and appoint Trump as president? Did Donald Trump expect the same thing? This is so illegal and unconstitutional that it leads us to regard this riot as a farce. Neither the ex-president nor his supporters understand the impact their actions have on others. They are immature people who take liberties with the truth and reality.

However, one must understand that it is western democracies that engender that kind of situation, for they are not based on reason. Politicians are not elected because they describe scientifically the actions that will solve certain problems. In fact, they charm voters, who want to be charmed. This political system encourages thus lie and manipulation.

Chapter 3: The negation of the truth and of the superiority of nature.

The nature of man is not to refuse to acknowledge the truth and the superiority of nature. If he does so, each insane individual that composes society, because of insane interactions, compels it to malfunction.

A- Crazy societies.

It is not easy to know the number of insane Westerners. In 2001 (1), the World Health Organization published statistics stating that 25% of all people in the world had suffered from mental or behavioral disorders at some point during their lives. The people who had written this report added that, in the world, 10% of adults suffered form this kind of disease. In brief, 25% of the inhabitants of planet earth had to be regarded as insane people, but they did not rave all the time, since 10% of adults were having a severe bout of madness.

In 2022 (2), the same organization published the same kind of report, which stated that in 2019 970 million people in the world suffered from a mental disorder, which represents 12,9%. A graph shows that 15,6% of Americans and 14,2% of Europeans are insane. Where do theses statistics come from? How are they gathered? Are they based on a sample of people or do they keep count of the whole population? It is clear that the information comes from governments since it is the different ministries of health that gather such statistics, and all governments do not proceed in the same way. For instance, in New Zealand, the Ministry of Health underestimates the number of insane people. In 2007/08, the district health boards saw 100 575 mental health clients, which represents only 2,37% of the population (3). In 2016 (4), 169 454 people consulted a mental health specialist, namely 3,6% of the population. Exact numbers do not imply that they delimit a phenomenon, all the more so because madness is a sniper. In some places, people do not see a physician because they don't want to be stigmatized. Sometimes they believe that they are sane, whereas they regard others as insane.

Besides, statistics do not reflect some mental disorders, for they are not severe enough to be regarded by societies, which are not sane, as pathological manifestations. The tip of the iceberg covers a maelstrom of little idiosyncrasies that prevent individuals from perceiving reality. There may be 10% of raving maniacs (psychotics), but how many misfits (neurotics) are there? Allow me to add that it is they who are the most dangerous, for they interact much more than psychotics do and thus propagate illusions very efficiently.

However, it is possible to evaluate the prevalence of madness in western societies if we correlate regional statistics. The ones will certainly enable us to correct the mistakes of the others.

In France, for instance, it is said that each year 13 million people suffer from a mental disorder (5); this represents 20% of the population, which seems to be a high rate, but it does make sense when we compare it with the suicide rate (1,32%), one of the highest in Europe, which proves that the French are quite unbalanced.

In the United Kingdom, in 2014 (6), one adult in six suffered from a common mental disorder, which excluded psychotic and bipolar disorders, autism, drug and alcohol dependence... Like the French the British are quite insane.

As for the Australians, in 2008, they began to document this phenomenon by asking people to conduct personal interviews at 14 805 private dwellings from August to December 2007 (7). They inferred from the data they collected that 45% of Australians aged 16-85 years had suffered from a mental disorder at some point in their lives and that 20% of Australians aged 16-85 years had experienced a mental illness in the past twelve months. In 2022 (8), they published other statistics, which confirmed what they had previously discovered: 43,7% of Australians aged 16-85 years had experienced mental illness at one point in their lives and 21,4% had suffered from a mental disorder in the pas twelve months. This high rate could lead us to believe that Australians are much madder than the French and the British, but it could also mean that what is regarded as insane in Australia is considered as normal in Western Europe.

It is more prudent to check the information thanks to American statistics, for, honestly, in that country, there is a tradition of measuring everything, which moves us to be less dubious about their figures.

In a report published in 2015 (9), it was written that 18,19% of American adults suffered from a mental disease. 3,77% of them declared that they had thought of committing suicide in 2014. In 2019, in the same kind of reports (10), one could read that 18,07% of American adults had mental health problems and that 4,04 % of them had suicidal ideation. In 2022, the mental health report (11) stated that 19,86% of American adults had experienced a mental illness in 2019 and that 4,58% of them had said that they had had serious thoughts of suicide.

At least the trend is clear, and there is no contradiction. Besides, these results are consistent with the percentages found by the French and the Australians. Hence, there is about 20% of adults who experience a mental illness each year. This figure would be the tip of the iceberg, and we would even infer from the Australian observations that around 44% of adult Westerners experience mental illness at least once in their lives. The outline of western madness would therefore be this impressive number, which leads us to understand why western societies are so dysfunctional. Let me play devil's advocate and add that we must also take into consideration a mysterious proportion of people who, for some reason, had not been counted.

Moreover, it is clear that all those unbalanced people are not deprived of their voting rights. In fact, in western democracies, very few people are not allowed to vote. Most of the time, they suffer from a severe form of psychosis and are institutionalized for lengthy periods of time, which means that many psychotics vote. Hence, we are to admit that a big part of western countries' electorate is composed of people who have difficulty distinguishing reality from illusion, which leads us to fully understand why western societies are so dysfunctional, but let us analyse qualitative data in order to refine this idea.

B- The third gender.

Whether you like it or not, Nature is your mistress, for it is she who bears you, and it is she who will kill you. A human's life is a long-lasting conversation with her, which is aimed at enabling individuals to attain their true nature: humanity bestowed upon them by reason. It is Nature who teaches you how to distinguish reality from illusion and good from evil. Hence, to negate her omnipotence is sheer folly. However, it seems that, in the Occident, some people are straining to acknowledge the gender which nature has bestowed upon them. It is true that sometimes she is a bit puzzling: when she decides not to show the difference between male and female.

In fact, what was called pseudohermaphroditism and could be called now sexual non-differentiation puzzled generations of western physicians. The French ones were not that bemused. In 1888, Tourdes (12) reported the case of a three-year-old child on whom an American doctor had operated in 1849 in order to remove his testicles because he did not have a penis, but a clitoris. Tourdes regarded this surgery as American eccentricity. In 1894, Émile Laurent condemned more vehemently this kind of behaviour, stating: "I consider that the so-called operations which are aimed at removing the penis-like clitorises of some women in order to turn them into flawless females who can make love more easily are immoral and unscientific." Unlike American physicians, 19th century French surgeons were not doctors

Frankenstein. They did not want to mimic God. Since the major organ systems worked properly (especially the urinary system) and the reproductive system was not diseased, they did not want to intervene, though, back then, France was a gender-segregated society.

The function of medicine is to cure, not to create things or change their nature or that of individuals. When a surgeon operates on an intersex child whose reproductive system is not diseased, he plays God: he resembles those Nazi physicians who wanted to improve the human race torturing the Jews. When Nature chooses not to determine the sexes, man has to accept her decision if the organs are not diseased. Moreover, the duty of physicians it not to comply with social habits which might be absurd. Physicians are scientists: they must stick to the rules of pathology.

It seems that, in the United States, physicians are inclined to operate on intersex people, and they don't always play fair. Actually, surgeries are performed when children are not old enough to evaluate the consequences of removing organs that produce hormones: they don't really understand that they will have to take hormones for the rest of their lives. Besides, parents are so stressed that they take all that surgeons tell them for granted, which is why they agree to let their children undergo an operation that will much affect their future.

In this regard the case of Kimberly Zieselman (13) is edifying. Although "he" was born with male chromosomes, his genitals were not visible, and his body was that of a female. Hence, he was raised as a female and ignored his genital peculiarity until he reached puberty. The absence of menstruation puzzled him and his parents. Examined by physicians, they discovered that he was genetically male, although he exhibited female characteristics. Following doctors' advice, his parents agreed to allow them to remove his healthy gonads. Kimberly was not aware of the whys and wherefores of the surgery. Now he must take hormones.

A certain child adopted by Mark and Pam Crawford underwent the same kind of surgery when he was a ward of court because his biological parents were not able to raise him. The operation was performed when he was sixteen months old (14). when the child was eight years old, he considered himself to be a boy (15). Hence, his adoptive parents sued the persons who performed and gave consent to that surgery. In 2017 (16), they won their case, and the state of South Carolina had to pay the 12-year-old child an indemnity for the moral and physical injury.

On the other hand, some individuals choose to change sexes; nobody compels them to do so. In fact, they refuse to obey the diktat of Nature. Their parents and society failed to match their sexualized bodies assigned to them by Nature with the role they had to play in society and in its continuation.

They refuse to acknowledge their sexes, but must we regard them as lunatics? French psychologists, at the end of the 20th century (17), did not dare to say that. In 1980, Daymas stated: "the transsexual individual who opposes biological reality is not ill. He or she does not suffer from transformation delirium like president Schreber. He or she does not wink at you like a perverted transvestite. He or she is convinced that he or she is right." In 1985, Castagnet (19) also declared that transsexuals are not psychotics, which does not mean that they are not neurotics, or immature people, or social misfits.

Hence, surgeons have been operating on them in order to match up their bodies with the gender they want to assume. Dora Richter might have been the first transsexual to undergo complete male-to-female genital surgery (the operations took place from 1922 to 1931). In 1930 and 1931, Lili Elbe, a Danish painter, underwent several reassignment surgeries. His body rejected the transplanted uterus, and he died of post-operative complications. Laura Dillon (20) was luckier. In 1939, she began taking hormones in order to masculinize her body. She had a double mastectomy in 1942, and then she underwent more than a dozen operations to construct a penis.

However, it is Christine Jorgensen who popularized transsexualism and that kind of surgery. In 1950, he began to take female hormones and soon underwent surgery. The shy boy who had striven hard to behave like a male when he was a US serviceman became a popular blonde babe in the US and in the rest of the world.

CITY EDITION

DAILY NEWS

NEW YORK'S PICTURE NEWSPAPER

4¢

EX-GI BECOMES BLONDE BEAUTY

Operations Transform Bronx Youth

A World of a Difference

"She" was interviewed, her face adorned the front pages of lots of newspapers, but all this did not prevent some American psychiatrists to declare that this kind of surgery was inappropriate because these people had severe psychological problems that did not disappear after the operation.

Nowadays, some American states, like Alabama and Oklahoma, try to ban gender-affirming treatments and procedures, but we don't know whether this policy will lead to a clear understanding of genders.

C- Gluttony.

Let us mix now quantitative and qualitative data together and analyse the spread of overweight across the Occident. Of course, since the proportion of old people in society is increasing, the rate of overweight people is also increasing, for the metabolism of the old, their individual hormonal balance and the difficulty of moving rarely allow them to remain slim. Besides, medical norms can be quite reductive because they do not take into consideration people's constitution. So we will not take overweight statistics for granted.

However, obesity, which is technically extreme overweight, is a factor whose meaning is easy to interpret. In fact, it almost always reflects the perversion of volition. Man must eat in order to survive, not because he enjoys it. When an adult is obese, we know that he or she has ignored the laws of Nature, which compels any individual to show temperance in order to stay healthy. When a child is obese, it shows that his or her parents and society have refused to educate him or her; this is sheer immorality.

Overweight is not a new phenomenon, especially because in some western countries traditional cuisine is not healthy. For instance, it is common practice for Spaniards to fry food, and the "croquetas" (meat of fish fritters) one can eat in Sevilla are partially responsible for the swollen bellies of the inhabitants of that city. Nonetheless, if the Spanish have always been plump, obesity was rare. Some figures (21) show that there is a sharp increase in the percentage of obese people: in 1987, 6,9% of adult Spanish men and 7,9% of adult Spanish women were obese, whereas 18,2% of adult Spanish men and 16,7% of adult Spanish women were obese in 2017. There is a strong correlation between theses figures and the rise of diabetes and hypercholesterolemia. Since the proportion of obese children remained constant from 1987 to 2017, one may attribute Spaniards' obesity to the sedentary lifestyle of Spanish adults.

As for Australians (22), there is an increase in the number of adults who are extremely fat (types II and III). In 1995, 5% of Australian adults were in that situation; in 2014/15, 9% of them were. However, all Australians are not subject to that phenomenon. In fact, Aboriginals and Torres Strait Islander adults are much more likely to be affected by obesity. One may say that there are insufficiently active and that they are lots of social factors, but there might also be physiological reasons. That being said, the number of obese Australian adults rose from 27,9% in 2014/15 to 31,3% in 2017/18; the period of time is so short that the behavioral factors must be regarded as predominant.

In some western countries, the obesity rate is extremely high. For instance, the prevalence of obesity in New Zealand adults is around 34% (23). In the United States, it is even worse: in 2015/16, 39,8% of adults were obese. In that country, obesity begins in childhood: in 2015/16 (25), 18,5% of US children and adolescents were already obese (5% of them were obese in 1971/74). The following graphs show a continuous rise in the proportion of obese Americans from the beginning of the 1960s to 2015-16. In 1960/62, 10% of men and 16% of women were obese, and in 2015/16, 37% of men and 40% of women were regarded as obese. As for severe obesity, it rose from 0% of men and 1% of women in 1960/62 to 5% of men and 9% of women in 2015/16. In summary, 71, 6% of Americans are overweight, and it is easy to determine the cause: it's gluttony!

Figure. Trends in overweight, obesity, and severe obesity among men and women aged 20–74: United States, 1960–1962 through 2015–2016

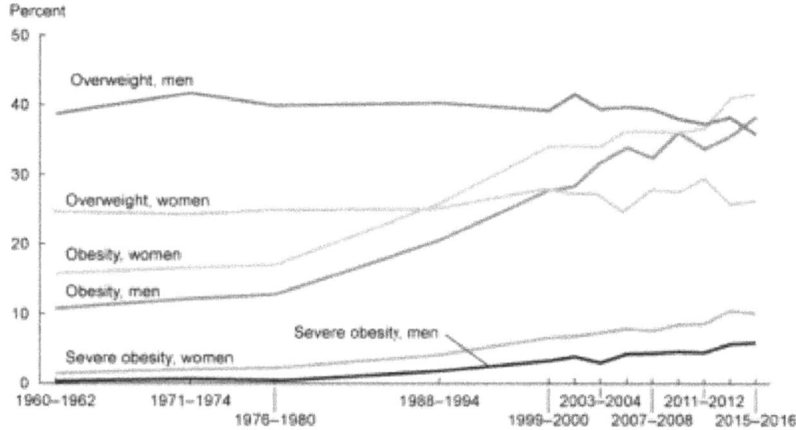

NOTES: Data are age adjusted by the direct method to U.S. Census 2000 estimates using age groups 20–39, 40–59, and 60–74. Overweight is body mass index (BMI) of 25.0–29.9 kg/m²; obesity is BMI at or above 30.0 kg/m²; and severe obesity is BMI at or above 40.0 kg/m². Pregnant women are excluded from the analysis.
SOURCES: NCHS, National Health Examination Survey and National Health and Nutrition Examination Surveys.

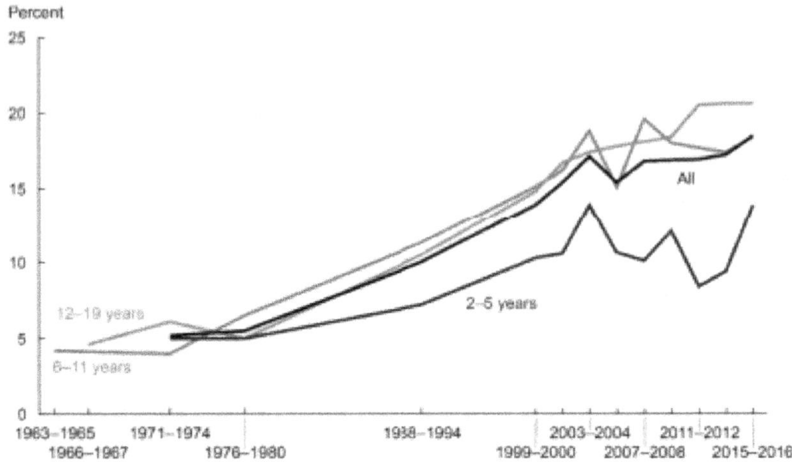

It is clear that the history of American cuisine is an accumulation of weird recipes that popularized unhealthy foods. Sugar and fats flatter the demanding palates of gluttons who do not want to understand that eating is not a pleasure, but a necessity. In fact, Americans absorb more calories than they used to. In 1970 (26), each American ate 2025 calories every day; in 2010 he or she absorbed 2481 calories every day. Of course, Americans eat more sugar, but, above all, they eat much more fat and grain than they used to. Since they are not more sporty than before, they gain weight and the whole nation exhibits its lack of volition as it shows its big belly to the rest of the world.

Part II: Man as the enemy of man.

Chapter 4: When freedom leads to imprisonment.

A- The origin of self-defense.

Man is not the enemy of man. People who believe that are lunatics, for humans must socialize so that they may reproduce. If they refused to do so, humanity would disappear. Hence, they are to regard others as partners. Sometimes they can even befriend them, and sometimes they must reject those who refuse to acknowledge that man is not the enemy of man, namely immature people and psychotics. Of course, sane, humane people must protect themselves from those dangerous individuals, but self-defense must not lead to individualism or indifference to others' plights: humans are humane because they care for people.

Some Westerners do not agree on that. Americans, for instance, are prone to individualism because of their country's history. The first settlers were confronted with adversity: they strove hard to grow plants, raise animals, find food, adapt themselves to different climates, tame nature, and live in peace with the native population. Thoreau's *Walden* is but the reasonable hope of a man who internalizes a society's struggle for survival. Hence, any American dreams of a pond, a cabin, a piece of land, and a gun. Self-sufficiency and self-defense are unshakable believes to which many Americans continue to subscribe.

The Revolutionary War strengthened them. Since all Americans had to fight the Britons, the law had to allow them to carry and use weapons in order to defend themselves and, at the same time, subdue the enemy. The second amendment to the US constitution legalized what was a common practise. The Americans established a militia composed of armed citizens whose aim was to protect the population, which is not a bad idea per se, but when those citizens were off duty, they were allowed to carry and use their arms, which is a very bad idea, for public order, by its very nature, must be maintained collectively since self-defense leads to disorder. The second amendment turned all Americans into potential avengers or mass murderers.

Consequently, many Americans own guns, all the more so because some of them are hunters or shooters. The number of hunters is quite stable (1). In 1960, around 15 million of hunting licenses had been sold; 15 938 891 of hunting licenses were sold in 2023. As to target shooting, it's not easy to estimate how many Americans practise this sport, for one does not have to register to shoot at a clay pigeon. According to the National Shooting Sports Foundation (2), in 2016, more than 20 million Americans spent money to participate in target shooting in the US. So, if we add the 20 million shooters and 16 million hunters together, 36 million Americans (10,58% of them) need a gun, which is the tip of the iceberg. In fact, many more Americans own a gun. It is self-evident that it's impossible to know the approximate number of gun owners because there are no statistics, and if there were, some people would not tell the truth. However, we can venture an estimate, for a few surveys were carried out.

According to Tom Smith and Son Jaesok, in 2014, 31% of Americans said that they kept a gun at home (3). As for Ted Van Green (4), in June 2021, he conducted a survey which shows that 40% of households possess a gun. There are disparities between country and city dwellers, for 53% of country households and 29% of city households possess a firearm. So, we can infer from this that at least 30% of American households own a gun, which surprises all Europeans since in Europe very few people are allowed to carry a weapon. There are a few shooters and hunters, but the regulation is so strict and they are so unpopular that governments prevent them form promoting their activities. Besides, the police fight against organized crime, which includes the search for illegal weapons. That's why there are not so many firearms in Europe.

Hence, it is little wonder that those weapons serve other purposes. Americans have been arguing for ages over the link between gun ownership and gun violence. Whatever the opinions, one must admit that a toothless, nailless lion is less dangerous than one that displays sharp teeth and nails! Similarly, a disarmed individual is quite inoffensive, though neither the despair nor the violence disappear. In fact, gun ownership facilitates crime.

In 2019 (5), 39 707 Americans died because of gun violence; in 2022 (6), the number increased drastically: 44 332 Americans died in that fashion. It is clear that most fatalities are due to suicides. In 2019 (5), suicides accounted for 60% of those fatalities and 54% in 2022 (6). In 2019 (7), 84% of firearm homicide victims were men; 53% of them were black men; young black males aged between 15 and 34 made up 2% of the population but accounted for 37% of all gun homicide fatalities. Such figures move people to purchase firearms to defend themselves, which shows that they distrust the police, others, and the regime!

B- Mass murder.

But what leads ordinary people to kill themselves or others? Let's say that sane people do not behave in that way. You may retort that war compels sane individuals to kill. I may tell you that they are not sane anymore, for one who agrees to surrender one's free will is not a sane adult anymore but an immature one: immaturity is not sanity!

However, hatred is a key component of a sane individual's personality. Its function is to enable a righteous person to implement a plan that is aimed at addressing a danger, which allows him or her to survive. This kind of hatred is reasonable because it is based on the accurate observation of reality. The humanity of the one who hates somebody will mitigate the effects of such hatred: he or she will not kill the person who strives hard to harm him or her.

As to psychotics' hatred of people, it is caused by fear. They fear men because they believe that they are as dangerous as they since they are supposed not to have control of their desire for murder. Hence, they try to kill the persons whom they fear. This sort of hatred is insane because it is unjustified.

The hatred experienced by immature people is a bit different. The very immature individuals whose egos are weak fear others because they believe that their narcissism harms theirs. Since they want to be proud, they intend to belittle others in order to prevent narcissistic erosion and strengthen their characters. Others are but objects that are deemed useful only if they enable them to consolidate their self-respect. When they decompensate (go mad), any person who is accused of belittling them is regarded as an enemy who must be killed. This type of hatred springs from an illusion and is thus unjustified.

On the 20th of April 1999 (8), two students at Columbine High School killed thirteen people and committed suicide. The police was unable to discover the reason for such a behaviour, but they investigated the matter thoroughly and provided much information, which shows that the two students were far from being sane people and that society was guilty of enabling them to find weapons and to perpetrate this abomination.

It is clear that Dylan Klebold and Eric Harris were deranged immature persons. Because of disabilities and his parents' incapacity to overcome this problem, Eric Harris had not completed the mirror phase (9), which means that he was emotionally unstable and very immature. He fought against depression and was on the verge of lunacy. As for Dylan, we don't know the reason for his immaturity, but we realize that he was quite depressed. Such people are not strong enough to handle the frustrations of life.

At the end of the month of January 1998, they tried to steal electronic equipment in a van. The police caught them, which traumatized them, especially Eric, who began to decompensate, which moved him to see a psychologist. His parents began to distrust him, which ruined his self-esteem. This parental rejection induced a nervous breakdown. So he received counseling and started to take antidepressants. I doubt that they were efficient, for many people noticed that his mood got worse. Patrice Doyle (10) declared that he began wearing black clothes and boots and became a loner. Scott Rathburn (11) pointed out that he became introverted and did not talk with people anymore. On the 13th of April 1999, Angel Pytlinski (12) noticed that Eric was severely depressed because his father accused him of talking LSD. This event was probably the factor that moved him to cross the Rubicon.

Meanwhile, he and Klebold strove to get weapons. Christopher Walker (13) refused to buy Eric a gun because of his dark side. In 1998 (we don't know the precise date), Judy Brown, the mother of a student, met Eric in a mall (14): he was buying a magazine. She was so upset that she contacted the police. In November 1998, Eric wrote in his journal (15) that he had arms. We don't know how he got them. Around March 1999, he bought propane tanks (15) in order to make bombs.

When unbalanced people are armed, it's never good news for society. The latter must never arm hatred, all the more so because sane people can go mad at some point, which nullifies all the policies that are aimed at preventing gun violence by means of prohibitions against selling weapons to insane people. If you really want to stop gun violence, you must prohibit guns. You should also prohibit bladed weapons and some dangerous implements. However, you will never stop violence, for, as I already said, it can be useful sometimes.

C- Lock them all up.

In order to mitigate the effects of violence, societies isolate violent persons for a while, for we all agree that prisons are not aimed at redeeming them. Unfortunately, prison comes after the crimes have been committed, which implies that they do not allow politicians to handle societal violence well.

The Americans must be nervous, for they are prone to lock up all criminals, including petty criminals. In fact, they set a gun in your hand, let you be exposed to temptation, and tell you not to misbehave or else they beat you up and send you to prison. I am sure that everybody would relax if less weapons circulated throughout the country.

Meanwhile, imprisonment is the rule, and behaviors as benign as jaywalking or sitting on a sidewalk can bring Americans to jail (16): low-level offenses account for about 25% of the daily jail population. For instance, if defendants fail to appear in court or to pay a fine, judges don't hesitate to issue a bench warrant for their arrest. In Europe, things are different: judges commission social workers to help litigants.

Similarly, illegal immigrants are locked up. Though they have infringed a law, they are neither criminals nor dangerous persons. However, when they are caught (17), they end up in a prison-like facility, where they will have to await deportation. Is this really necessary? Besides, 33% of the persons who are in jail have not been convicted (18), which means that they may be innocent.

All prisoners are not petty criminals or innocent people, but one realizes that social determinism is at work. Actually, people of color – who face much higher rates of poverty – are overrepresented in the American prisons and jails. For example, Black Americans account for 12% of the US residents but 38% of the incarcerated population. As you can see in the following graph, prisoners are always poorer than non-prisoners, black male prisoners are poorer than the white ones, and Hispanic female prisoners are poorer than all the others. It seems that the incarceration rate of women has risen faster than that of men because of financial obstacles such as their inability to pay bail.

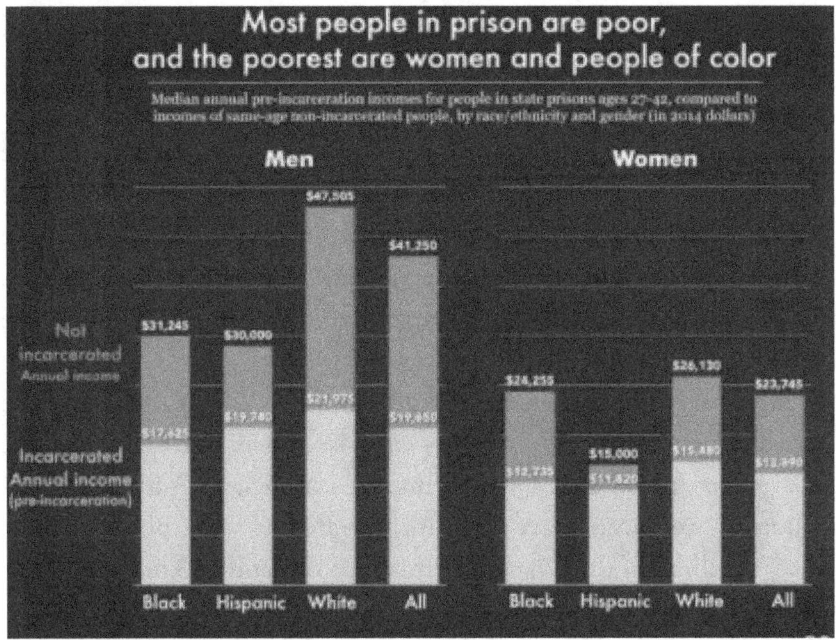

Hence, American prisons and jails are a key element of a social regulating system that separates the poor from the rest of society, re-establishing racial and social segregation. In this Orwellian world, inmates are compelled to work (20) so that they may afford basic necessities like medical visits and hygiene items. The whips have disappeared, not the slaves!

On the other hand, this system is quite inefficient, for 82% of people incarcerated in a state prison were arrested at some point in the ten years following their release (21). 69% of people imprisoned for a violent offense are rearrested within five years of release. However, only 44% are rearrested for another violent offense.

Consequently, the US are the country with the highest incarceration rate. In fact, 0,63% of Americans are in prison (22), whereas 0,35% of Turks, 0,33% of Russians, and 0,24% of Chinese are incarcerated. Besides, 22 000 Americans are involuntarily detained or committed to state psychiatric hospitals and civil commitment centers (24). Many of them are not even convicted, and some are held indefinitely. 9 000 are being evaluated pretrial or treated for incompetency to stand trial; 6 000 have been found not guilty by reason of insanity or guilty but mentally ill; another 6 000 are people convicted of sexual crimes who are involuntarily committed or detained after their prison sentences are complete. Are those institutions hospitals or illegal prisons? Is American psychiatry a science or a method used by the government to detain certain people illegally?

In the US, imprisonment is commonplace. As you can see in the following graph (25), the number of prisoners is but the tip of the iceberg, for prison has a major impact on society. Actually, if 4,9 million of Americans have been incarcerated at some point in their lives, 79 million of them have a criminal record and 113 million adults have an immediate family member who has ever been to prison or jail, which accounts for 43% of American adults. In fact, the US are a science-fiction police state, a paranoid society that fears itself! Those people pretend to foster liberty, but they strive to lock it up! I had forgotten that the bronze statue that faces New York is not American but French!

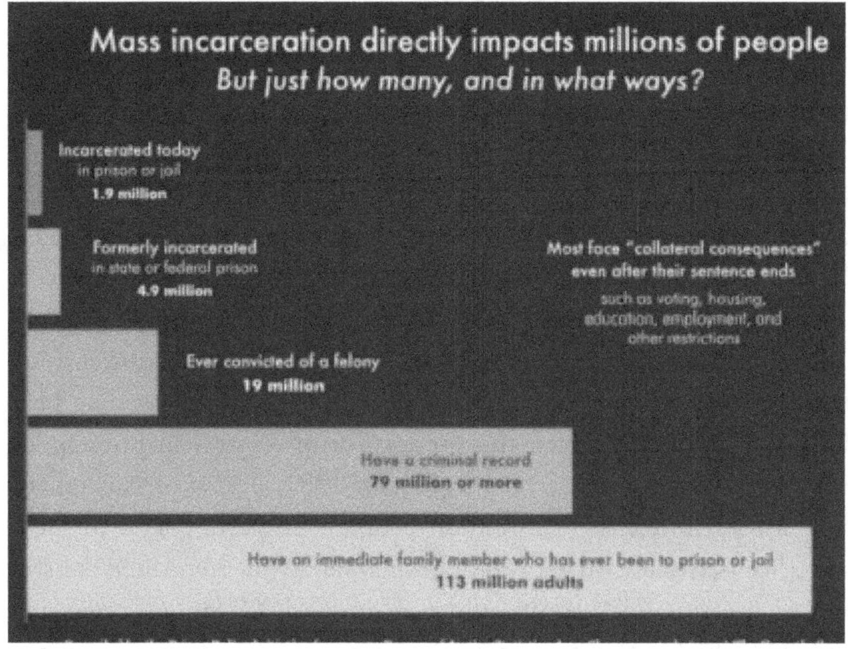

D- The Australian experiment.

Westerners are not doomed to live in countries where everybody fears everybody because of the number of guns in circulation and of gun-related homicides. The British (26) demonstrated that citizens and governments could agree to implement policies aimed at almost banning firearms, although there was a tradition of hunting.

In Australia, similar measures were taken after two massacres. The first one occurred on the 28th of April 1998 at Port Arthur, in Tasmania. A man who had a personality disorder killed 35 persons and injured 23 others. The second one took place on the 21st of October 2002 at Monash University, in Melbourne. A student killed two people and injured five others. The gunman was acquitted of the crimes due to mental impairment. The population was so shocked that the government felt morally compelled to restrict drastically the number of firearms. Nowadays, an Australian must hold a firearm license, which is granted to people only if they demonstrate that they have a real reason to hold one, which does not include self-defense (27). The laws forbid insane people and offenders to obtain one. Besides, the government controls the importation of certain weapons that may lead to massacres (like semi-automatic rifles) and it organized a gigantic firearm buyback.

It took place between October 1996 and September 1997 (28). The authorities collected around 650 000 guns, which at least enabled them to disarm some of the persons who were not allowed to bear firearms anymore. In fact, the proportion of Australian households with a firearm as fallen by 75% (29). In 1997, 6,52% of Australians held a firearm license (1,2 million people); in 2020, 3,41% of them were licensed gun owners (868 000 people). However, there are still lots of firearms in Australia: there are around 3,5 million registered firearms, which makes an average of 4 guns for each licensed gun owner. However, the proportion of Australians who hold a gun license has fallen by 48% since 1990. Furthermore, less criminals and insane people are allowed to bear a firearm, and less semi-automatic guns are in circulation.

Consequently, it is little wonder that the government succeeded in pacifying Australia. The number of mass shootings (30) decreased drastically. So did the number of people murdered by a gunman (31): 76 Australians were killed in that fashion in 1989/90, 59 in 1999/2000, and 23 in 2020/21.

Gun homicides in Australia from 1989 to 2018.

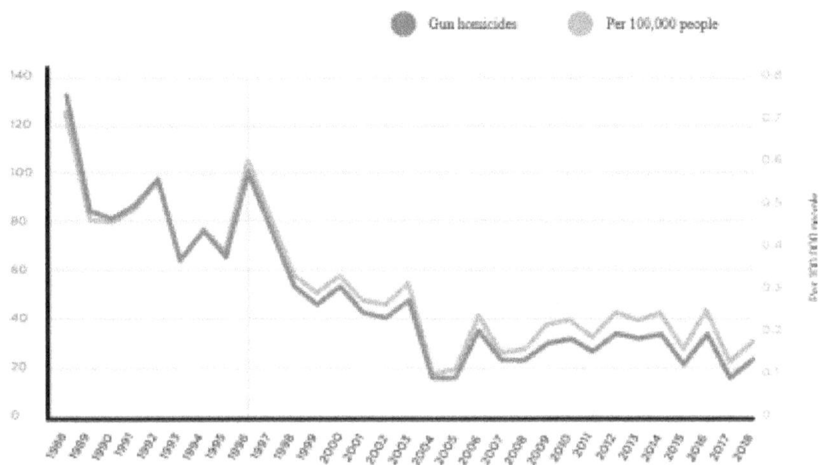

This may lead you to believe that nowadays Australians don't use guns to murder people but bladed weapons, which is true since in 2020/ 2021, for instance, 79 out of 210 persons were stabbed to death, whereas 23 were shot dead. However, the government regulation induced a decrease in the number of homicides. In fact, 307 people were killed in 1989/90 (which accounts for 1,81 per 100 000 people), 351 in 2001/2002 (1,80 per 100 000 people), 227 in 2014/2015 (0,95 per 100 000 people), and 210 in 2020/2021 (0,82 per 100 000 people).

As to the link between the measures and the suicide rate (32), it is not easy to establish one. Of course, less people commit suicide using a gun, but as you can see in the following graph, if in 1996 there was a slight decrease in the number of men who killed themselves, women keep on committing suicide. That being said, the aim of such policies is to prevent innocent people from being killed or harmed by others, and they proved to be efficient. Since suicide is but self-harm, the social implications are less important.

Suicide deaths by sex in Australia form 1991 to 2021.

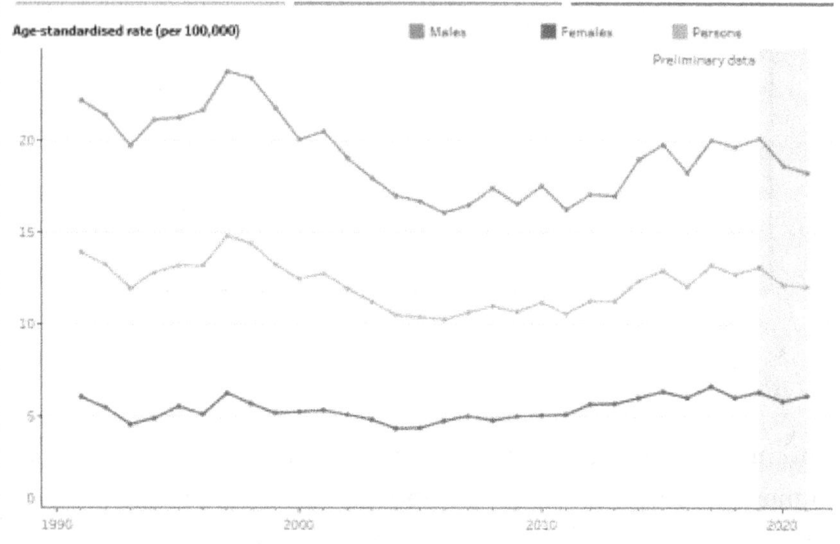

Chapter 5: Perpetual racism.

Racism is not a concept that can accurately delimit what people experience when they reject someone because of his or her ethnicity. Truth to tell, there are several types of racism, which depend on the level of intelligence of individuals. In fact, a person whose personality is organized at the psychotic level does not perceive the outer world like immature people or those with Neurotic Personality Organization. Consequently, when we refer to racism or other feelings, we should always specify the personality organization of people. That being said, it is hard to determine which part of the population influences social attitudes the most. Personally I don't think that psychotic racism exists, for psychotics' perception of reality is so distorted that they don't categorize humans according to ethnicity: they hardly know how to individualize themselves. On the other hand, immature people keep distinguishing races. Since western societies are mainly composed of immature persons, it is little wonder that racism is a widespread phenomenon, all the more so because reasonable people (namely those whose personalities are organized at the neurotic level) can be quite racist.

A- The good white colonists.

However, western societies have not always been racist, which demonstrates that history is a key factor. Actually, when the European merchants (like Marco Polo) and explorers (like Christopher Columbus and Magellan) met foreigners, they were more intrigued than afraid. When they conquered those exotic lands, they even had to befriend them in order to survive. For instance, the Spaniards favored intermarriage because all the conquerors were men and had thus to do so in order to start a family. The Spanish aristocracy behaved in the same way, for they believed that it would be easier to rule those territories if they married the daughters or sisters of the ex-rulers: same-class marriage was the rule.

As for the French, they were fascinated by exoticism (1). In 1766, two years before James Cook, the chevalier de Bougainville began a journey around the world. The expedition reached Tahiti in April 1768. When the first islanders approached the ship, he noticed that the women were pretty: he described them as nymphs. He even named the island "New Kythira", as if it were a kind of paradise. On the 6th or 7th of April 1768, Bougainville and his officers came ashore in order to see whether there was some water. A great meany Tahitians approached them, touched them and undid the buttons of their jackets so that they might see their bodies. Bougainville was not afraid. He was the first European to describe the Tahitians. He writes that there are two races. The first race is the most beautiful one. The men are tall and strong; he compares them to Hercules and Mars. He even asserts that they are not that different from the Europeans, even though the color of their skin is dark. The second race is characterized by a smaller size and curly hair. He does not say that they are ugly; he just writes that they are not as handsome as the former and adds that they are smarter. Bougainville's book was a huge success, and it gave birth to the mythical vahine: a comely dark-skinned lady who bewitches all fair-skinned Frenchmen.

Many years elapsed, and France became a refuge for certain persons who experienced racism in certain western countries. For instance, Josephine Baker did not hesitate to move to France so that she might not be treated like an inferior anymore (2). When she was a child, she was always afraid, for white people kept barking at her. Besides, she knew that a poor black girl would have difficulty prospering in a country that had institutionalized racism. When she arrived in France, she was not regarded as a second-class citizen anymore. Since racial segregation did not exist, she could go wherever she wanted and mix with whites. Then she became a famous vaudevillian, joined the resistance, fought for the end of racial discrimination in the US, was inducted into the Pantheon on the 30th of November 2021, and is thus regarded as a "great Frenchman" now!

In fact, the US were and still are a perfect example of colonialism. The history of that country has structured the mind of generations of Americans. The early American colonists struggled to produce food, and they often starved. Neither the wild animals nor the Native Americans were always hostile, but they were always regarded as arch-enemies because there was fierce competition for food, especially meat. Hence, the newcomers stole lands, woods, fish and buffaloes from the "Indians". Those persons were faithless predators who were preoccupied by their survival. As their situation improved, they realized that the organization of world economy allowed them to exploit black slaves. Actually, slavery is but the domination of the workforce by capital owners who are too mean to pay workers' salaries. A white supremacist like Dixon (3) was fully aware that black slaves were docile workers who enabled the white planters to remain wealthy. The other justifications for racism were aimed at reinforcing the main reason.

However, the US were a democracy, and in such countries, there are always some people who believe that all the inhabitants must have equal rights. So the progressive northerners fought the conservative southerners and defeated them, but the level of racism did not decline, which is quite puzzling. In fact, contemporary racial discrimination against black people is but the perpetuation of the colonial class struggle, which is rooted in the 17th century struggle for survival. Some white Americans are convinced that, for their own sake, they must remain their social inferiors, all the more so because there is some competition for certain jobs and a lot of Latin Americans who emigrate in order to get them. This kind of cast system is a means to secure jobs, and the most efficient way to perpetuate it is to keep on segregating students, for the whites who attend the best private schools will get the well-paid jobs that will enable them to send their children to the same schools: it is a vicious circle. Hence, the other racial groups are doomed to poverty. Sometimes Racism is a class struggle.

Nonetheless, African Americans rebelled and campaigned to end racial segregation, which is the rule nowadays. As a matter of fact, the different ethnicities keep on distrusting one another; they live in different neighborhoods, attend different schools, frequent different places, and think differently. The country that was formed by a constant flow of immigrants resembles 18th century Europe: the most snobbish Americans pride themselves on being descended from the first settlers, the Englishness of their forebears ennobles them, and the whiteness of their skins is a license to despise all the dark-skinned "newcomers". The US are not a nation but an accumulation of particularities that make it difficult for citizens to acknowledge that people are equal, though they are different. Different people may have different views, but they must accept the truth and be willing to live in the same place, which induces compromises.

In that country, the white policemen are trigger-happy: they keep on killing black people who are not always guilty of an offense. The antagonism between whites and blacks is evidenced by statistics, which separate anti-white racist incidents from the anti-black ones (4). One notices that the level of "recorded violence" is steady and persistent. Certain persons would even venture to say that it rises, but we must be cautious about this kind of data, for it is quite subjective and the calculation is not that accurate. However, one realizes that the American Civil War is not over and that this nation is stuck in the past.

As to Australia, it is also a place that was colonized by white people, and colonial racism is still a feature of Australian society. It is less visible than the American one because it has never been legalized: the whites never got along with the Aboriginals or the Torres Strait Islanders, but they did not pass a law on racial segregation. In fact, Native Australians are not numerous (5): they are overshadowed by other ethnicities, especially the white ones. However, there is much distance between Aboriginals and the whites, and even today (6) many of them say that they often experience racial prejudice. Truth to tell, they believe that they are treated with less respect than others. Sometimes whites insult them (7), yell at them, and are afraid of them. Sometimes the police bother them. Once again, the settlers from Europe turned the natives into social inferiors.

Moreover, other ethnicities experience racism. According to a 2020 survey (8), 31% of Chinese Australians declared that they had been called offensive names, and 18% of them said that they had been physically threatened or attacked because of their ethnicity. Actually, Australia is a continent under siege: the inhabitants, the government and the police strive hard to limit immigration. It is self-evident that lots of Asians try to settle down in Australia and that Australian society wants to remain white and occidental.

B- The spectre of Nazism.

The Occident gave birth to the worst kind of racism, namely Nazism. The causes were psychological and historical. Actually, society is mainly composed of immature people, whose reactions determine its nature. Those people's personality organization is incomplete. They don't bear frustration. They fear others because they believe that they are going to belittle them, which leads them to become loners and prompts them to find means to protect themselves from them and their opinion of them. They overreact when their egos are endangered, keep looking for an ideal self that will boost their self-esteem, and lose touch with reality or reject it, for they don't possess the concepts that would enable them to discover it, and they refuse to acknowledge the truth when it may harm their self-esteem. Immature persons are problem people who create problematic societies. The Occident is mainly immature, which is why it is problematic.

Historical factors enabled immature people to institutionalize their hatred of foreigners. Actually, Europe has always been a patchwork of cultures, races and nationalities, but the French Revolution (especially the Napoleonic era) moved governments and peoples to unite so that they might protect themselves and live according to rules that reflected their cultures. Although most European countries were monarchies that prohibited free elections, monarchs fostered national customs, did not go against their subjects' believes, and created countries that were linguistically and culturally homogeneous; the multicultural Austrian Empire was thus regarded as an aberration. Hence, Otto von Bismarck unified regions where people spoke German, which included the east of France. When the Germans lost the First World War, the French recovered those territories, which prompted the Nazis to conclude the process of German unification by conquering the regions inhabited by German speakers, which included Austria. At long last they got what they named Lebensraum (vital space).

Besides, the economic crisis led the Germans to regress and find ways to survive. Not only had some strangers (especially the French) deprived them of certain necessities, but all of them were viewed as their rivals. Consequently, the many Jewish immigrants were made the scapegoats for the Germans' plight, all the more so because they were very different from them. The Nazis advocated racial purification because it is a method which immature persons employ so that they may avoid depression.

Since Germany was a democracy, the majority of unbalanced immature people voted for the Nazis, who came to power effortlessly and legally; this would have never occurred if Germany had remained a monarchy. Moreover, the shenanigans of politicians and help of certain sane persons facilitated this. For instance, Hjalmar Schacht, who became Economic Secretary to the Treasury and was a person with an obsessional personality (9), not an immature one, collaborated with them, though he had almost nothing in common with them: he was a Freemason, a cosmopolitan, a democrat, a humanitarian, a Christian and an educated person who considered that Hitler was but a "half-educated man". However, he shared his views on certain national matters and ended up regarding him as an intelligent person, though he was aware of his limitations as a human being and that evil was not absent form the pact he had made with the Nazis. He had compromised his principles, and since he was sane, he was the guilty party.

I think that almost all the members of the Nazi government were amoral immature people, which is why they implemented the policy on the extermination of the Jews. The Holocaust was supervised by Himmler (10). The Reich Minister of the Interior signed so many documents and made so many decisions that one may doubt Hitler's culpability. In fact, in 1943, Hans Heinrich Lammers, who was Reichsminister and the chief of the Reich chancellery, heard that the Jews were being killed. He asked Himmler whether this was true or not. Himmler denied that there were legal killings. Then he asked the Fuhrer the same question, who repeated what Himmler had said about the absence of legal killings. Nevertheless, Lammers believed that Himmler knew that he would come, which is why he had arranged that Hitler would say the same thing. It is clear that Himmler concealed everything and kept manipulating everybody. He was a crank who wanted to destroy Christianity, humanity, and people he regarded as "subhumans".

Nazism and antisemitism still exist because there are still people who are very immature. In France, extreme antisemitism resurfaced in 2006, when a young Jew was kidnapped, tortured for three weeks, and then immolated (11). French historians have not recorded many acts of violence as barbaric as this one. All things considered, it was the most barbaric crime committed in France between 1946 and now. In fact, Youssouf Fofana – who was born in Paris and lived his whole life in France – plotted to kidnap Ilan Halimi with the help of a group of his acquaintances whom the media called the gang of the barbarians.

We don't have any information about Fofana's youth, but the psychiatric report made by Françoise Toulouse-Sylvestre shows that he is a remorseless criminal, a narcissistic uncompassionate psychopath who lacks insight and self-criticism, a predator, a manipulator, a vainglorious, paranoid man who misinterprets many things and keeps attributing the feelings he does not like in himself to people around him. In other words, she describes a psychopath who is on the verge of lunacy.

In order to earn money, he chose to kidnap Ilan Halimi, but his family could not afford to pay the ransom. Consequently, he and other members of the gang became more violent as time passed. Zigo, who was only seventeen, kept beating him. He was the most impulsive, brutal and inhumane of them all. The kidnappers never called Ilan by his name; they turned him into a thing and refused to speak to him and even to touch him: they wore gloves, as if they wanted to protect themselves from a disease!

A few year later, on the 11th of March 2012 around 8 O'clock in the morning, Mohamed Merah killed three Jewish children and a Jewish teacher in a school located in Toulouse. He was the product of a dysfunctional family: his father was a drug dealer and his mother could not raise her five children because no man helped her. She was so overwhelmed that she contacted the social services. Mohamed was sent to an institution, and a document dated August 18, 1997 (he was nine) shows that, at home, the situation was problematic. When he was fourteen, he was very aggressive: he kept insulting girls, stealing, destroying goods and assaulting people. He refused to comply with requests from adults: he was the typical psychopath. At the age of sixteen, he became a bit more sociable, but he already led a double life: during the day he worked in a garage, at night he stole cars and committed robberies. His psychological evaluation was performed in 2009 (he was twenty). The psychologist pointed out that he was nervous and that he took sleeping pills and psychotropics in order to calm his anxiety. He had formerly tried to hang himself and had stayed in a psychiatric hospital from the 25th of December 2008 to the 8th of January 2009. However, he was in tune with reality, what he said was logical and his brain's processing speed was high, although he had difficulty with abstract thinking. He was depressed and suicidal. The psychologist concluded that he was an emotionally immature individual.

Racist incidents recorded by the French police.

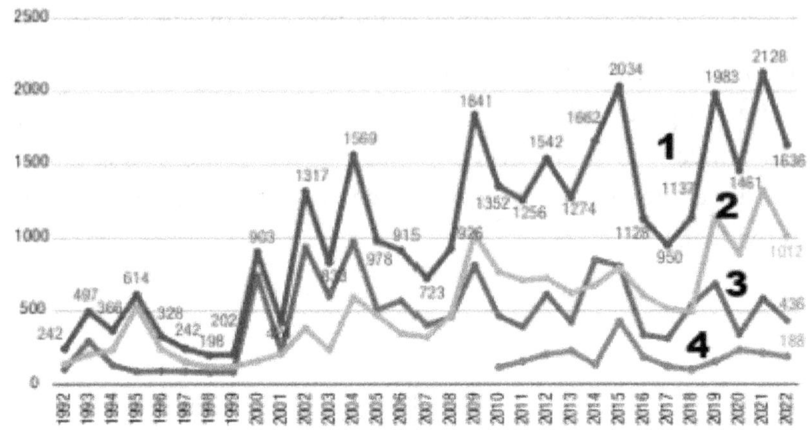

Line 1: All racist incidents.
Line 2: Other racist incidents.
Line 3: Antisemitic incidents.
Line 4: Islamophobic incidents.

Actually France is a dysfunctional, diseased society. I daresay the French Jews' situation is worsening. As you can see in the graph (12), the number of antisemitic incidents (line 3) rose in the year 2000, and the situation remains steady. Many French Jews worry (13), which is why many of them move to Israel. Besides, one notices that racism is spreading in that country (line 1), which proves that the French are regressing.

In western countries, there are lots of weirdos who come out of the woodwork when racial tension mounts. They demonstrate, wave Nazi flags, display swastikas, shout, and riot sometimes, but the disturbances are manageable. Actually, Neo-Nazis have not formed organizations that are powerful enough to destabilize governments. However, some of them are dangerous terrorists who can harm society.

On the 22nd of July 2011, Anders Breivik (14) detonated a bomb outside the building housing the office of the Prime Minister in Oslo and murdered 77 members of the Socialist Party on the island of Utoya because he blamed them for harming the Norwegian race and Christian civilization.

Anders Breivik claimed that he was not a racist; he just wanted to protect his race from the Muslims who were allowed to settle down in Norway by the socialist government, which is why he killed the young socialists who would rule the country someday and perpetuate this policy.

I don't know whether we must regard him as a typical Neo-Nazi, but it is clear that he is a white supremacist, for he believes that white is beautiful and feels proud of his ethnicity, though he does not extol blond hair, fair skins, or blue eyes. He advocates the selective breeding of genetically pure Scandinavians, who can be found in the north of Sweden. The full-blooded Aryan is replaced by the full-blooded Scandinavian. The veneration he felt for the Nordic race impelled him to have plastic surgery to change the shape of his nose. His is not that racist, for he wrote that the only way to save the Christians in the Middle East was to form an alliance with the Jews: he is not anti-Semitic but Islamophobic.

That being said, he, too, is an immature man. When he was four (15), psychologists met him. They said that he kept to himself, that he was passive and fearful, and that he gave monosyllabic answers. His childhood shaped the strange relationship between him and women, and one realizes that he suffers from castration anxiety. For instance, he wrote that he was feminized by the Norwegian feminist society, especially at school, where feminist teachers try to create "beta-males", not "alpha-males". According to his half-brother, he does not dare to make contact with girls; he thinks that he is a little afraid of them. In fact, the relationship between him and his mother was dysfunctional. For various reasons, no man interposed himself between him and his mother in order to show him the difference between genders. Many years later, he had difficulty understanding what a man is. He was still trying to develop his gender identity and build his personal identity, which led him to fight against what prevented him from achieving that. The racism exhibited by immature persons has a lot to do with personality disorders.

C- Suspicion.

There are mild forms of racism, which resemble suspicion. For instance, Europeans prefer certain peoples, which has something to do with history and cultures. A recent study (16) suggests that in Denmark and Sweden people who bear Middle-Eastern names have much more difficulty getting a job than the natives of those countries. In Belgium (15), recruiters underrate dark-skinned applicants. In Austria, they underrate applicants whose ethnic backgrounds are Serbian, Turkish, Chinese and Nigerian. In Finland (18), Austrian immigrants are preferred to the Polish ones. Honestly, when whites disparage other whites, this is not racism but inherited distrust. The European Union is a patchwork of nations that fought one another for centuries. The Second World War resulted in the exacerbation of nationalism, which led almost all Europeans to hate the Germans, who committed unspeakable crimes, and the Poles, who helped them. All European students learn this from their history textbooks and are as suspicious of them as their grandparents were. The European Union did not erase the memory of the tragedy, although it was based on reconciliation between all European peoples. Actually, this strange federation is aimed at preventing war in Europe by debilitating the nation-states, but this policy is backfiring: nationalism, regionalism and particularism are rising.

Besides, Europeans distrust gypsies, who were allowed to settle down in Western Europe when Romania joined the European Union. They are popular neither in their homeland nor in the rest of Europe, for they are seen as thieves. The Parisians dislike them because lots of Gypsy girls stroll along the platforms in the underground in order to search discretely travelers' pockets for purses, wallets and mobile phones. In general, the French distrust them, which is evidenced by the annual report on racism (19). In fact, around 67% of them consider that the Gypsies do not try to integrate into French society.

As for the Britons, for various reasons, they don't really like the Poles. Actually, the two peoples ignored each other for centuries; when the British needed workers, they did not ask the Poles to move to the UK, for the French were a more appropriate workforce: they fulfilled tasks which the English did not enjoy (catering), were not that Catholic, had not killed too many Jews during the war, lived in a country the Britons like, were almost their neighbors and spoke a language that resembled theirs. Moreover, other persons, who came from the United Kingdom's former colonies, were well acquainted with the Briton's ways and spoke English. Hence, they were employed in other industries.

In May 2004, Poland and other western countries joined the European Union. The British government allowed those foreign nationals to settle down in the UK so that they might work in industries that did not attract enough British workers (catering, the construction industry, transport, and certain public services). Because of unemployment, low wages and lack of opportunities in Poland (20), hordes of Polish workers moved to the UK, and there was cultural tension. The British are used to spending time with foreigners and tolerating other cultures, but when the UK was a member of the European Union, it was invaded by European immigrants. Nowadays, very few people speak English in London! If we don't know how the Poles or other Europeans behaved, we know for a fact that they were regarded as people who deprived the British of jobs, welfare services and housing.

Besides, some Polish workers behaved as if they were in a conquered territory. On the 27th of August 2016, two of them provoked a group of English adolescents (21). They were manifestly intoxicated and might have made racist remarks, which kindled the youngsters' wrath. An argument ensued. Then a short fifteen-year-old boy punched a tall strong fourteen-year-old Pole, who fell to the ground; his head hit the pavement hard, and he died. The murderer told the psychologist who evaluated him that he wanted the victim's family to know that he was not a violent person and was deeply sorry. When foreigners live in a country inhabited by people they don't like, they should behave themselves.

Racism can be engendered by people's dislike of certain religions. Since Henri IV's reign, the French have separated religion from public matters, and they have rarely been suspicious of Islam: in 1536, François I even entered into an alliance with Muslims, which shocked all European Christians. As time passed, they conquered Muslim territories and governed Muslims. It is self-evident that the decolonization of Northern Africa made it difficult for the French to regard Muslims as friends. However, since the 1960s, a great many Muslims who were born in the Maghreb have settled down in France.

So Islam is not an uncommon religion anymore and the French know Muslims very well, but do they often befriend them? Not really, for, most of the time, they befriend people who resemble them! French society fears heterogeneity. Besides, Islamic terrorism has led the French to view them with suspicion.

In 2014 (22), 48% of them considered that they did not try to integrate into French society. In 2022 (23), if 32% of the French declared that Muslims did not try to integrate into French society, 42% of them believed that Islam endangered French civilization, and 75% of them said that women who used to wear a burka were social misfits. In fact, peoples that have known Muslims for centuries are beginning to dislike them. Even the Spanish, who are not Islamophobic, are becoming suspicious of them. For instance, in February 2000, the inhabitants of El Ejido rioted because two Muslim emigrants had killed three persons. Xenophobia is aroused by facts sometimes.

Chapter 6: The conflict between genders and that between generations.

A- The conflict between gender.

The place of women in society has never been a comfortable one. Since they are smaller and weaker than men, most of them have always considered that they are superior to them. The Palaeolithic Period turned men into hunters, who provided the community with the main source of energy: meat. Women just picked fruit and vegetables, which were secondary foods. The one who held the spear that prevented starvation kept it in order to subdue those who tried to deprive him of the elements that enabled his tribe to survive. The spear holder thus became the warrior who maintained law and order. Since then, he has not let go of the weapon that ensured his supremacy.

As time passed, societies became more sophisticated: the chief of the tribe turned into a god-king who prevented the universe from collapsing. His wide shoulders held the skies, his strength was regarded as a major quality, and the virile king has to beget a muscular son who would inherit his father's kingdom and duties. To achieve that goal, the king's divine semen had to take shelter in a womb which guaranteed that the future king was really his son. Hence, women's sexuality was controlled by men, all the more so because most of them wanted to bequeath their estates to their true sons and children. In fact, religion institutionalized the ruling class's opinion. Females became perpetual sinners whom men had to take care about so that society might remain as it was.

Besides, immature men aggravated women's social inferiority. Behind all the laws and customs that turn them into perpetual children, there are always unbalanced, immature Anders Breiviks (19), who regard them as enemies of men. They accuse them of preventing them from becoming men. Their gender is a poison they want to get rid of. Their so-called impurity is a venom that might lead them to suffer from depression. Since all societies are mainly composed of immature individuals, immature men keep on belittling women, although lawmakers try to mitigate the effects of such behaviors.

Consequently, in European societies, women keep on being social inferiors who are poorer than men. In general, in the European Union (2), women earn 12,7% less money than their male colleagues. Actually, a third of women have a part-time job, versus 8% of men, which means that they usually stop working in order to raise their children or take care of a relative who is sick. Besides, when European women grow old, the gender pay gap widens. Actually, a great many of them are in low-paid jobs. In 2021, only 34,7% of them were senior executives. Hence, when they retire, they are much poorer than men: in 2020, the pensions of the European women who were aged 66 or older were lower, on average, by 28,3%.

As for American Women, they are not luckier than the European ones (3). In 2022, they earned 82 cents for every dollar earned by men. Of course, their situation improved, for, in 1982, they earned 65 cents for every dollar earned by men. Although they generally begin their careers close to wage parity, they lose ground as they grow old, and college-educated females are not exempt from this fate, for all women can become mothers, which explains why mothers aged from 25 to 44 are less likely to be in the labor force than fathers of the same age. Moreover, American women are rarely well paid, for they don't often become senior executives, and those who are not WASPs are in a worse situation than they: in 2022, Black women earned 70% as much as white men and Hispanic women earned 65% as much.

From that it follows logically that western women are still striving hard to be elected. There is parity in politics in New Zealand (4), and the Swedish, the Norwegian, the Danish and the Spanish are close to achieving this. However, in many western countries, like France, the United Kingdom and the USA, politicians are mainly men. In the US, for instance, in 2023 (5), 28% of the "congressmen" were women, 12 out of 50 governors were females, and in cities of 100 000 inhabitants and more, 26% of municipal positions were occupied by them.

Moreover, western women are often mistreated by men: this kind of demeanor reflects certain men's mental disorders. In the US, 1 in 4 women (6) experience sexual violence, physical violence, or stalking by an intimate partner during their lifetime; 1 in 5 women are victims of rape or attempted rape during their lifetime. In Australia (7), in 2016, 1 in 5 women experienced sexual violence. In 2023, the Australian Institute of Criminology carried out a survey about partner violence experienced by women in Australia in the first 12 months of the COVID-19 pandemic. The cases of 10 000 women were studied. 9,6% of these women experienced physical violence by partner, 7,6% sexual violence, and 32% emotionally abusive, harassing and controlling behaviors. Western women are still mice tortured by cats. When western males regress, they cannot control their feelings anymore, and they become brutal psychopaths who regard all women as objects whose aim is to satisfy their desires. The history of the relationship between men and women is but an endless fight between immature men and women who fear one another, which impels them to try to manipulate and disarm one another. Since women are almost always weaker than men, they are almost always their prey.

European women are also mistreated by men. According to a 2014 survey (8) that gathered information about 42 000 women from 28 European countries, we estimate that 7% of European women aged from 18 to 74 experienced physical violence in 2013, and 2% of them experienced sexual violence. In fact, between 24 and 39 million European women (which accounts for 13% and 21% of them) were sexually harassed in 2013. The authors of the report added that, in general, one out of three European women have been sexually harassed in their lifetime since the age of 15.

Spaniards have been fighting for years against violence against women. In 2011 (9), 32 242 Spanish women were assaulted by men, whereas 32 644 Spanish women were assaulted by men in 2022, which shows that there is no notable evolution. It seems that there is a hard core of violent men who are unable to redeem themselves. The women who are most often attacked by men are aged between 25 and 34, and they often know their attackers: 23% of them are married to or divorced from them, and 43,8% of them are their partners.

However, some European women are more mistreated than the Spanish ones. The figures regarding the Scandinavian ones, for instance, keep puzzling observers. The Swedish authorities even noticed that there is a growing number of women who say that they have been sexually harassed (10). Some scientists researched this issue (11). They perused the Swedish Crime Registers from 2000 until 2015 and gathered information about 3 039 men, aged from 15 to 60, convicted of aggravated rape. 47,7% of the offenders were born outside Sweden; 34,5% of them came from the Middle East or Northern Africa, 19,1% from Black Africa, 15% from Eastern Europe, and 14,4% from Asia, which demonstrates that the authorities were so naive that they allowed dangerous men to immigrate to their country. 40,8% of the rapists were born in Sweden of Swedish parents. 15,9% of them suffered from mental disorders, 21% were junkies, and 19,3% were alcoholics. Hence, in a country where gender equality has become a reality, women are as mistreated as in countries where they regard them as their inferiors, for, whatever the place, when there are lots of men who are emotionally or mentally unstable and who undervalue them, they keep on raping and attacking them. Besides, one wonders whether those Scandinavian men who advocate gender parity believe that they are their equals in the private sphere (12). In fact, sexuality implies that men are "enterprising" by nature, which tends to complicate the relationships between men and women and prevent equality of the sexes in certain circumstances.

B- The conflict between generations.

It is self-evident that wealth is usually an attribute of old age, which is why there are always young Don Juans who crave for their parents' property and would like to bury them as soon as possible. However, the conflict between generations that is taking place is much more serious than what it was before, for the prior generations' turpitude turned them into devils: they destroyed civilization in Verdun, crucified mankind in Auschwitz, beheaded democracy in Vietnam and are killing the earth itself. When young people hate them, they have reason to do so.

Baby-boomers (people born from 1946 to 1964) belong to a generation that is still in power in western countries. In the US (13), they are on average about ten times wealthier than millennials (people born from 1981 to 1996), they are overrepresented in positions of economic power, they form a major, highly reliable voting bloc, and they dominate both state and national politics. Besides, many of them continue working, though they have reached retirement age, which prevents younger generations from getting the well-paid jobs that would enable them to amass money. Millennials are particularly upset because they are poorer than prior generations at the same age, which is why they perceive baby-boomers as the biggest threat to their generation's interests. Conversely, baby-boomers perceive millennials as the biggest threat to their interests, all the more so because they also accuse them of disregarding American values.

In the United Kingdom, this intergenerational conflict shows up in elections (14). In fact, a growing number of young people vote for the Labour nowadays. In 2010, 31% of persons aged from 18 to 24 voted for the Labour; in 2019, 62% of them voted for the Labour, whereas 64% of the oldest electors voted for the Tories. The intergenerational conflict is becoming a class struggle: the young tenants want to dispossess the old landlords!

The situation is even worse in France, for the phenomenon is amplified by the structure of the housing market. In fact, the older generations purchased houses when the prices were low (from the beginning of the 1960s until the middle of the 1980s) and inflation was high, which enabled them to pay back the fixed-rate mortgages easily. Most of them now own a flat in the most expensive areas of large cities and a house in the sought-after holiday destinations. Many of them are landowners who lend at least one apartment to young professionals, who strive hard to pay the rent, all the more so because lots of baby-boomers still occupy positions of economic power, which prevents them from getting well-paid jobs. Besides, the French retirement system is financed by taxes on salaries. Hence, the intergenerational conflict has been institutionalized, and all politicians are aware that they will never be elected it they don't perpetuate the system. For instance, the people who voted for the baby-faced Emmanuel Macron were mainly grandmas and grandpas, who believed that he would allow them to keep their privileges. They were right, for the did not change the logic of the retirement system, and he rose the pensions.

In this country, the young are the servants of the old, and they are much poorer than they. In 2002, 8,2% of people aged from 18 to 29 were poor (15); in 2018, 12% of them were poor. Conversely, in 2018, 3% of people aged 75 or over were poor, whereas 4% of them were poor in 2008. The figures speak for themselves! This rouses a feeling of rebellion in the young, which the French don't really want to acknowledge. The last report on this issue (16) shows that some interviewees fear intergenerational tensions, but the study is so imprecise that one is under the impression that the young and the old get along with one another.

Fortunately, reality (I mean the 2023 summer riots) enables us to discover the truth. In fact, on the 27th of June 2023, Nahel Merzouk, a lad who lived in Nanterre, was killed by a policeman, which moved many youths to riot for several days. Did they want to protest against the murder of the lad? The official report (17) shows that 91% of the rioters who were brought to trial were men; 79% of them were born in France. According to the police, most of them were of North-African and sub-Saharan descent. 29% of the culprits were eighteen and nineteen years old; 44% of them were aged from 20 to 24. 29% of them did not have a diploma; 38% held a middle school diploma and 23% a high school one; 22% were students and 36% unemployed people. 226 out of 395 culprits had never been convicted of a crime. They rarely said why they had taken part in the riots or pillaged stores. Only 8% of them declared that they wished to avenge Nahel Merzouk's death. Most of them just wanted to fight the police, whom they hate, and were influenced by their peers. Those who pillaged the stores were either well-organized professional thieves or opportunists mobilized by the social media. Actually, those young adults are a kind of angry lumpenproletariat that steals what it cannot afford to buy from the wealthy. On the one hand, there are young executives who long to overthrow the Gerousia that prevents them from getting what they deserve; on the other hand, there are youths who live in a society that turned them into outcasts who are compelled to steal (from the old) what might enable them to regard themselves as human beings; all of them hate the old!

A bank branch vandalized in July 2023 (18)

Part III: Economic issues.

Chapter 7: Mass unemployment and poverty in the Occident.

Liberalism did not result in full employment and wealth, and the industrial revolution showed that although modernization enabled workers to work easily and more efficiently, it reduced the number of jobs, for fewer hands could produce more goods. Since the dawn of humanity, workers had had the upper hand because demand had always exceeded supply.

At the beginning of the 19th century, the Britons realized that all those machines were stealing their jobs. So they protested, and the king had some of them hanged. Since then, nobody, not even the most radical communists, has dared to question mechanization. In fact, they keep saying that "robots" cannot harm employment, for the jobs that are destroyed in factories are created in research units, but all steel works cannot become engineers in two shakes of a lamb's tail.

In the Occident, the 1973 oil crisis was a traumatic tsunami in that regard. Factories relocated in countries where the workforce was cheap, which compensated for the surge in energy prices. Deindustrialization was toxic. Unemployment and the attendant poverty surged in Western Europe. Although some countries, like Germany, were able to overcome this thanks to the development of innovative value-added products, others were not, and they are still enduring Asian competition, which is why their unemployment rate has become structurally high. However, non-Westerners regard some parts of the Occident as a promised land, and they keep on trying to emigrate to

Europe and the US. It is clear that those persons, who believe that they will find a well-paid job, will rarely integrate into the western economy and societies.

A- Poverty in Europe.

In fact, nowadays, Westerners strive hard to earn their living, for the new international division of labor compels the Occident to follow rules that link it to countries whose costs of production are much lower, which destroys jobs in the West. Even the "Swedish socialist paradise" had to comply with economic liberalism, which led to scarcity of employment and poverty.

According to Eurostat, in 2018, 16,4% of Swedish people were poor and 1,6% very poor (1). The impoverishment of Swedish society accelerated during the 2008-2018 period. Besides, these statistics do not include homeless persons; there might be 33 250 of them (2), which accounts for 0,32% of the population.

Single parents are peculiarly subject to poverty (3), for, in 2013, about 30% of them were poor. Welfare state retrenchment impoverished people who were already in a precarious situation since, by their very nature, they could not count on their partners to address the vicissitudes of life. Moreover, although in-work poverty is less stringent in Sweden than in other European countries (4), it is not insignificant. In 2017, for instance, 6,9% of the Swedish working population lived in income poverty, whereas 9,4% of the EU workers were in such a situation. Needless to say, temporary employees, part-time workers, people with little qualifications, and migrants were doomed to in-work poverty. Actually, in 2019 (5), 4,5% of Native Swedes and 14,8% of foreign-born Swedes who were in work were poor.

In 2022 (6), because of inflation, a growing number of Swedes frequented Matmissionen: eight charity supermarkets that are supplied with food by producers and retailers who donate it because it must be eaten shortly or its appearance is not that great. The members of Matmissionen can purchase goods at at an affordable price. The number of members rose from 7 200 persons in January 2022 to 14 700 in October 2022. Consequently, Sweden is not a safe haven from liberalism-induced poverty.

As to France, it was peculiarly hit by mass unemployment and poverty. From 1980 (7) to 1986, the job losses in the industry amounted to 100 000 every year and to 165 000 every year from 1992 to 1993. Meanwhile, the tertiary sector, especially trade, which guaranteed job growth since the 1970s, stopped hiring. Hence, the unemployment rate surged to 12,5% in 1994, part-time contracts became the norm, and poverty increased. Each economic crisis worsened the situation, excluding a growing number of weak populations from employment, namely the young, the old, women and unqualified workers. In 1994, 5% of the workforce never worked and 5 million French people lived below the poverty line.

Since then, things have not changed. In 2018 (8), 8,3% of the French were poor. That being said, the young were much poorer than the old, for 22,3% (9) of people aged from 18 to 29 were poor, whereas 4,7% of persons aged 75 and over were in the same situation. The handicapped, people without a diploma (10), immigrants (11), unemployed persons (12), single parents and people who lived alone were often poor (13). The impoverishment of French society is confirmed by the level of illiteracy (14): we estimate that 7% of French people aged from 18 to 65 cannot read or write, although they all went to school, which means that their cultural background is that of poor people who are not used to educating themselves and who are ashamed to seek support.

In French overseas territories, the situation is much worse (15). For example, 53% of people living in Guyana, 42% of those living on La Réunion and 33% of those living on La Martinique are poor, which makes them resemble poor countries. In this regard Mayotte is a part of France that does not look like the Occident at all. It is a kind of hell since 77% of the inhabitants live below the poverty line, which is a source of tension,

In southern Europe, poverty and mass unemployment are not new phenomena. Since the second part of the 19th century, there were waves of migration from Spain, Portugal, Italy and Greece to norther Europe and the United States of America. In fact, southern Europe industrialized partially, which did not allow it to amass enough money to fully benefit from the subsequent phases of economic modernization and growth. Consequently, the unemployment rate remained high and poverty keeps on harming society.

In Spain (16), in 1972, 2,5% of Spaniards were unemployed, 5% in 1976, 22, 5% in 1985, 25% in 1994, and 11,84% in 2023 (17). Hence, the unemployment rate is structurally high; so is poverty, but there are regional differences. In fact, the inhabitants of southern Spain, especially Andalusia, are much poorer than the Spaniards who live in the north of Spain, which reflects the economic disparities between the industrial north and the rural south that strives hard to keep on growing fruit and vegetables since water is becoming expensive and rare. For instance (18), severe poverty affects 8,9% of Spaniards and 14,4% of Andalusians.

Moreover, persons who have a pension (which includes retirees) are much poorer than persons who work. In 2022 (19), 35,8% of them lived below the poverty line and 14,7% were extremely poor. Actually, extreme poverty is gaining momentum: the rate surged from 3,6% of people in 2008 to 8,1% in 2022 (20).

B- Poverty in the US.

As for the Americans, they have never been fooled by capitalism. In fact, they are convinced that liberalism is the only civilized way to set up societies because they worship freedom, which is but an illusion. Consequently, they strive hard to combat any kind of communism (I mean economies controlled by the state), but they also take liberties with free trade. Truth to tell, they are ready to implement any plan so that they may sell their products all around the world, and they never hesitate to protect their domestic market, for they are aware that too much liberalism is always detrimental to job growth and national wealth. Americans are not capitalists but protectionists, protectionism being another sort of communism.

Actually, this nation was traumatized by the Great Depression, which is why the American government keeps intervening in the economy. Although the rest of the world hates the Americans because of that, protectionism is quite efficient, and all administrations succeed in helping the economy and keeping the unemployment rates quite low. As you can notice in the following graph, it is always a bit lower than in the rest of the Occident if we exclude the COVID-19 period, which is irrelevant.

The unemployment rate in the US
from the early 1950s to 2023 (21).

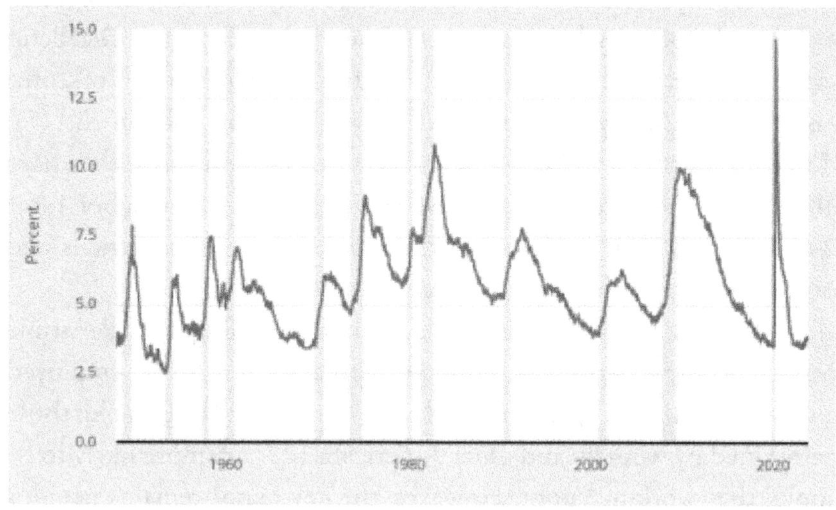

The Biden-Harris administration, dare I say it, achieved a goal that any Keynesian state would like to achieve: full employment.

That being said, full employment does not always bring wealth to the nation. Although the poverty rate declined from 1959 to 1969, there are always more than 10% of Americans who are poor (22).

Poverty rate in the US from 1959 to 2022.

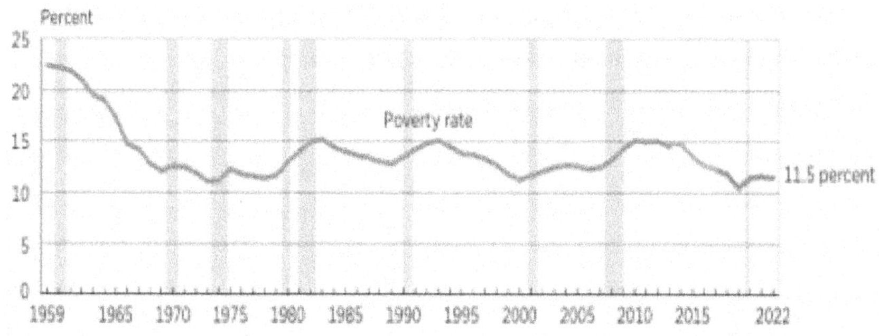

It is self-evident that workers' salaries do not always enable them to be above the poverty line. In the US, like in the rest of the Occident, certain laws allowed factories to move to places where the workforce was cheaper (23), which destroyed well-paid, stable jobs in the US. Moreover, since fewer American workers carry union cards, they have difficulty negotiating their salaries. Hence, 31,9% of the labor force (24) earns less than $ 15 an hour. Besides, house prices, rentals and bank fees impoverish people who are already poor (25).

The profile of the poor in the US is not surprising (26). Part-time workers, women, persons without a diploma, those who are employed in service occupations, families with children under 18 years old, those maintained by women, and older Americans (27) are more likely to be among the (working) poor. However, the key factor remains people's ethnicity, which keeps them in certain social classes.

Actually, American Indians and Alaska Natives are the butt of the joke (28). They have been estranged from American society for centuries and keep on being the first to suffer the consequences of economic crises. For instance, in April 2020, during the COVID-19 pandemic, the unemployment rate for them peaked at 28,6%. Then this rate declined and was 11,1% in January 2022, which is still much higher than the rate of 4% for the overall population. In general, 10% of them are unemployed, whereas the average is around 5%.

Unemployment rates for American Indians and
Alaska Natives and for the total population,
from January 2003 to January 2022.

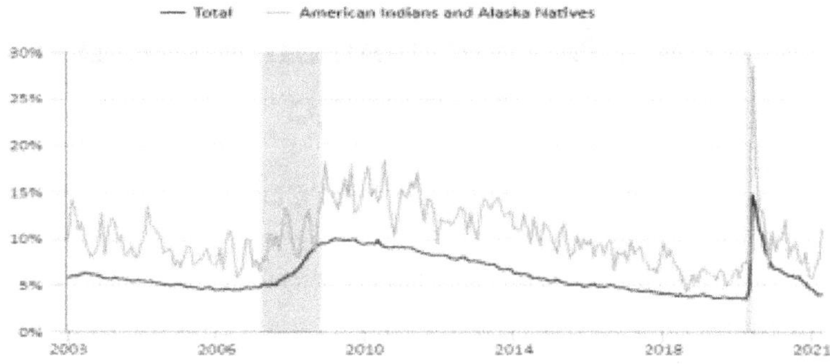

Black people and Hispanics are also more often unemployed (and poor) than Asians or white people (29). 46,2% of Hispanic workers (30) and 47% of the Black ones earn less than $ 15 per hour. Logically, the regions with the highest poverty rate are those where there are lots of African Americans and Hispanics, namely along the Mississippi River (31). In fact, Mississippi's Black residents are three times more likely to live in poverty than white residents. In Tunica County, 68% of Black families live in poverty and 23,8% are unemployed, whereas 12% of white families are poor and 2% are unemployed. However, its seems that the situation is improving, for although 10% of African Americans were unemployed in 1975, only around 5% of them were unemployed in 2021 (32).

Being a woman, especially a Black, or a Hispanic, or a Native American woman, dooms people to poverty (33) since 39,9% of self-identified women in the workforce and 50% of self-identified women of color make less than $ 15 an hour. On average, Black women are paid 64 cents to the dollar earned by white men, whereas Native American women are paid 60 cents and Hispanic women 57 cents. In brief, in the US, books keep on being judged by their covers!

Chapter 8: Overconsumption and the pillage of resources.

A- The illusion of consumption without consequences.

The industrialization of the West is not a new process. In fact, it started at least during the Roman period, when, in some regions, lots of slaves produced a great many pots in an industrial way. I mean that the models were homogeneous, that at least a part of the work was mechanized (the reliefs were molded out of clay), and that it was done on a large-scale basis. At *La Graufesenque*, for instance, archaeologists discovered a huge kiln in which 40 000 vases could be heated for hours at a constant temperature (1050°C.), which prevented them from cracking during the firing. Then they were sold throughout the Roman Empire.

However, technological advances and the use of new sources of energy allowed the Britons to increase the production of goods that were getting more and more sophisticated. For example, the spinning mule, which was patented in 1779, eclipsed hand spinning because a water-powered machine was able to work better and longer than man, who, suddenly, lost his superiority and became the obedient servant of tireless, omnipotent automatons. In 1785, thanks to an efficient steam-powered atmospheric engine, coal replaced water as the main source of energy, which allowed textile factories to operate almost anywhere, all the more so because trains soon provided them with coal in remote places. Besides, unskilled workers could easily manipulate machines that produced kilometers of high quality fabric in two shakes of a lamb's tail. In fact, the United Kingdom was covered with railways, which shortened the distance and enabled heavy goods' transportation as this released dangerous chemicals into the air. Industrial centers were so polluted that at the end of the 19th century the first environmental organizations were formed.

Then industrialization spread across Europe. France, Belgium, Germany and Sweden became important industrial centers. So did the United States. In this country, the process began in the valley of the Blackstone River, where a great many textile mills operated and turned the cotton grown in the South into mass-market products that could be purchased by a growing number of greedy consumers.

Greed is as human as envy and gluttony. Besides, democracy is based on equality; I mean that since all humans are equal under the law because hereditary privileges don't exist anymore, they believe that they, too, will become rich. The American dream, which is characterized by the idea that a poor immigrant will achieve a certain level of wealth, is but a democratic dream. Hence, after the American Civil War, when the US became a genuine democracy, since slavery was abolished, the American citizens, their wives and their children began to covet the great many goods (1) that confirmed that the wealthy European aristocracy had been sacrificed upon the altar of equality of opportunity. All of a sudden maids became princesses when they purchased costume jewelry and butlers at least grandees when they bought a silver watch. The millions of poor immigrants who populated the US came from European countries where scarcity was hereditary and class struggle their fate. In the US, they could at last become human beings who could lead the life they had chosen to lead and try to be well-off in order to persuade themselves that they, too, were persons of quality. Moreover, purchasing American products led those newcomers to believe that they belonged to a dignified family. They had abandoned the motherland – a kind of bad mother – which prevented them from maturing; they had cut the umbilical cord in order to reach the fatherland which assured them that they would keep deriving pleasure from the materialistic American society.

That being said, it is clear that all democratic countries prompt citizens to overconsume goods, for the aim of any democratic government is to ease tension. Democracies cannot stand to much inequality and poverty, for if they did, this would lead to a non-democratic society, a kind of plutocracy, which is profoundly aristocratic. Actually, if all citizens cannot be wealthy, they must at least believe that thanks to the regime they belong to the so-called "middle class", which destroys poverty and wealth in order to ease tension and homogenize society. All democratic governments strive hard to enrich voters so that they may remain in power and perpetuate the system. Hence, the good government is the one that makes you richer; overconsumption is therefore the logical consequence of such a situation since not all people behave like Uncle Scrooge, and they tend to buy goods in order to indulge themselves and acknowledge that they are richer than before.

It is self-evident that this encourages consumption and thus begets a social disease called consumerism. In fact, people must consume what they really need. In the West, citizens are but junkies who derive fallacious pleasure from buying products that lead them to believe that they are, in a way, like everybody and superior to non-Westerners, who are regarded as destitute persons who should comply with the western model of materialism in order to be happy. Ownership becomes everybody's raison d'être. Personally I think that Westerners are but crazy hoarders who accumulate rubbish because they are so immature that they believe that they will protect themselves in that fashion from the vicissitudes of life; those dreamers are sissies who are so narcissistic that they have lost touch with reality.

B- The plunder of natural resources.

Man has always observed nature in order to make use of it and survive. The primitive hunter-gatherers feared it as much as they exploited it, and they did not bother to steal what they should have produced. Then they invented agriculture, but they kept on regarding it as an endless source of materials, energy and wealth. Hence, they extracted clay, stones, metals and hydrocarbons, which contributed to the birth of European industry during the Roman period. It is clear that if ancient men knew that they could exhaust certain metals in certain mines, thew were not aware that their predating behavior had consequences.

That being said, it is not they who originated global warming because of the release of carbon dioxide gas into the atmosphere. In fact, during the Industrial Revolution, the demand for cheap, efficient energy compelled the Britons to use great amounts of coal in place of wood to power steam engines and smelt iron. The products they sold to the whole planet and which enriched them released vast quantities of carbon dioxide, poisoned populations and gradually elevated the temperatures of the atmosphere. The other European nations copied the Britons, and, for instance, at the beginning of the 20th century, the Belgians, the Austrians, the French, and especially the Germans became large coal producers and consumers. They also dug for iron and other metals that composed the products which facilitated the development of the West: railways lacerated lands and hordes of locomotives made hordes of greedy consumers suffocate. The Industrial Revolution is a massive failure, for it instituted the use of materials that endanger mankind.

Then the internal combustion engine replaced the steam engine. The spread of the use of petroleum aggravated the situation, all the more so because individuals were reluctant to change fuels and to use their cars less. Hence, Westerners and the rest of the world keep on bleeding the earth and polluting the air. The Americans are still large crude oil producers, and the petroleum and gas industries make up 8% of the US GDP, which is why they keep on drilling wells, although international regulations compel nations to implement plans aimed at reducing the consumption of fuel. However, if the Trump administration disregarded the Paris Agreement, in 2021, President Joe Biden rejoined it.

In fact, man is so greedy and imprudent that the whole planet is too small to provide him with the resources he needs to survive. As you can see in the following graph, nowadays, mankind uses more resources than the earth can offer; we need 1,75 earths to sustain Westerns' way of life.

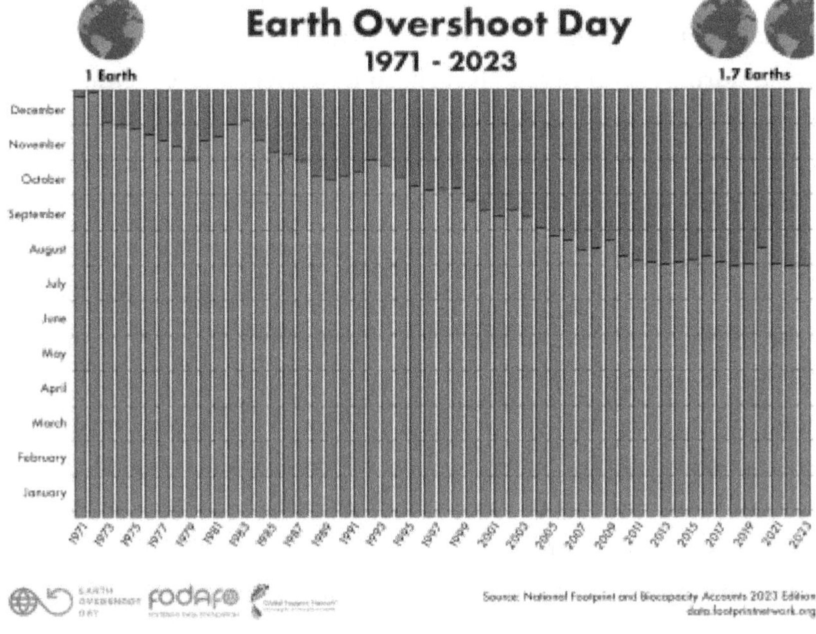

A suburban, individual house, two cars per household, air conditioning and heating, the water in the swimming pool, lots of plane journeys, and too many useless gadgets are illusions Westerners cannot afford anymore.

Actually, in the 1970s, they behaved in the same fashion, but it was not a major problem, since they were not numerous enough to endanger the planet. Besides, not all Westerners were that extravagant. Nowadays, in order to sustain their way of life, they compel farmers (including those who live in the Third World) to overexploit the earth. Consequently, agriculture accounts for 80% of world deforestation, it uses 70% of available fresh water, and 52% of world's arable land is degraded. Moreover, since they eat meat, a large part of the lands must be reserved for the production of food for animals. In the European Union, at least 50% of the cereal crops are consumed by farm animals, which is mismanagement, for there are already proteins in cereals. Honestly, it is stupid to produce large quantities of plant-based proteins in order to produce fewer quantities of animal proteins, which are not always that healthy, for they are often combined with saturated fat. People should eat less meat, all the more so because most of them are not allergic to plant-based proteins.

As to energy production, Westerners strive hard to provide alternatives to fossil fuels. In fact, other sources of energy have been in use since the dawn of humanity. For instance, geothermal energy is not a novelty, since hot springs have been used since Paleolithic times and the village of Chaudes-Aigues, in Central France, has been heated by geothermal hot water since the 15th century. Nowadays, Iceland and New Zealand are places where geothermal energy supplies a significant share of the electricity that is generated. However, this source of energy is not that eco-friendly, for geothermal power plants emit gases (carbon dioxide, hydrogen sulfide, methane and ammonia) that contribute to global warming and whose quantities are not always negligible. As for wind, it is less problematic since it can be regarded as clean energy. As a matter of fact, if windmills were widely used, in the 1930s, to generate electricity on American farms, it was the Dutch who, after the 1973 oil crisis, began to systematize wind power by means of the first megawatt wind turbine. Since then, the wind power industry has steadily expanded in the Occident, as did hydropower, solar energy and nuclear power. The latter is a much-criticized source of energy since accidents and the storage of nuclear waste are issues that are not easy to address. Actually, we automatically donate our nuclear waste to our children, grandchildren and descendants, for if the radioactivity it contains decreases by 99,5% after 100 years, the more intensely radioactive short-lived fission products decay into stable elements in 300 years, which means that it is they who will have to solve the problems we caused. Besides, certain events (mainly Chernobyl and Fukushima nuclear accidents) keep reminding us that nuclear power plants are complex entities. However, in some parts of the Occident, since nuclear power is cheap decarbonized energy, it is the main source of electrical energy. In France, for example, it accounts for more than 70% of electricity generation.

On the other hand, electricity is not that eco-friendly, since, at times, it must be stored in batteries, for electric cars, which are regarded as paragons of virtue, are in fashion in the West. It is clear that if the electricity that powers them comes from dirty energy, they are not eco-friendly at all. Besides, even when that's not the case, batteries have an impact on the environment, which is not negligible, since the extraction of lithium (3) and cobalt (4) requires a lot of water (in places where it is scarce) and only 5% of them are currently recycled. This is not the solution, all the more so because cobalt and lithium mining releases a lot of carbon into the atmosphere and cobalt is a metal that is quite rare. Hence, Westerners and all humans will have to invent other fuels to power their cars in an eco-friendly way.

C- The immediate consequences.

The survival of mankind relies so heavily on energy and natural resources that man is fated to keep on plundering the earth and making mistakes. Truth to tell, the need for gas and petroleum led oil companies to explore the bowels of the earth and thus to head into dangerous territory. The industry first moved into shallow water. Then technological advances (5) enabled oil platforms to drill under great distances under the water and the sea floor, but operating in such a situation was far more hazardous than on the continent. Consequently, in the 1970s, many oil platforms blew up; the most catastrophic accident occurred in December 1970, when Shell's platform B exploded in the Bay Marchand area: it took 136 days to bring 11 wild wells under control (6).

The prices of oil and gas always moved the gas industry to develop their business or to cancel their exploration operations. For instance, in 1985 and 1986, oil prices collapsed (7) to $ 10 per barrel, which led to the cancellation of most projects in the Gulf of Mexico, but when the prices rose again (8), from 2000 to 2010, western gas companies drilled frantically for oil. Moreover, in 2002, 2004 and 2005, hurricanes had a major impact on offshore infrastructure: hurricane Katrina destroyed 47 oil platforms (9) and damaged another 20, whereas hurricane Rita wiped out 66 oil platforms and broke up another 32. However, the most dreadful event is the explosion of Deepwater Horizon semi-submersible mobile offshore drilling unit, which occurred on the 20th of April 2010.

On that day and on the following ones, the crew (10) lost control of the well, which resulted in the release of liquid and gaseous hydrocarbons into the Gulf of Mexico, the explosion of the drilling rig, and the loss of 11 lives. On the 19th of September 2010, the Macondo 252 well was declared dead (11). They estimated that the volume of oil discharged during the spill amounted to 4,9 million barrels (12). This oil slick damaged considerably the wildlife along the coasts of Louisiana and in the Gulf of Mexico. The reports (13) showed that there had been errors of management and communication, but, above all, that in a complex environment humans were prone to lose touch with reality, which prevented them from acting thoroughly. In other words, the more complicated the system was, the less they could handle it.

As a matter of fact, the oil and gas industry almost always pollutes the environment (14), even when it operates onshore wells, for even when the abandoned ones are plugged, they often leak a bit of methane. Hence, it is little wonder that exploited wells leak much more methane than the abandoned ones. A study shows (15) that in 2016, in the parts of the US where there are lots of oil wells (namely Texas, Wyoming, Colorado, North Dakota, Pennsylvania, West Virginia and Southern California), people suffer more from asthma. Scientists studied childhood asthma and they discovered that the exacerbation of the disease was linked to the presence of nearby wells or to the dominant wind that carried pollutants (methane, non-methane volatile organic components, oxides of nitrogen, sulfur dioxide, fine particle, and ammonia). Besides, the offshore oil and gas industry can have an important impact on the marine environment (16), but the situation improves when oil spillages diminish. Two sediment and fauna surveys (17) conducted in 2015-2016 in the Fladen Ground and in the Mid North Sea High showed that the concentration of pollutants in the sediments had improved over time (from 2001 to 2015) and that diverse seabed communities did not seem to be affected by pollution.

As to coal mining, it releases sulfur dioxide, nitrogen oxides, carbon monoxide and fine particulate matter (18), which aggravates the symptoms of asthma in places where there are coal mines. Although no survey has been conducted, one can be sure that there must be more asthmatics near such places and in the rest of Australia. Australians should consider this problem, but mining is so important to Australian economy that the government is not in a hurry to discover what it would like to ignore. However, radioactivity being a major issue, it conducted a survey (19) in the area of the upper South Alligator River, for there were lots of radioactive wastes that dated back to the 1950s and 1960s. Scientist gathered water mussels and discovered that they were not very radioactive. In fact, it is not uranium mining that is dangerous but an accident at a nuclear power plant, which can release dangerous levels of radiation over an area.

Chapter 9: Westerners confronted with climate change.

A- Inaction or reality denial?

It is not the first time man has been confronted with environmental problems. I often refer to the end of the Old Kingdom, when drought began to turn the Egyptian savanna into a desert, which affected crops and reduced the stock of meat. I guess that famine compelled people to steal food and to pillage tombs in order to get valuables that were used to purchase food. Gradually, as drought deepened, they broke the rules that had enabled society to function. The authority of the god-king was being questioned; the emaciated bodies could not bear children anymore; morality was defeated by the struggle for existence; authority was subdued by necessities; the Old Kingdom vanished into thin air.

However, the process lasted for generations, and what is happening now is much more sudden. Hence, one can wonder whether mankind will be able to overcome this problem, all the more so because climate change denial prevents people from acknowledging the truth and thus tackling this crisis.

It is clear that Americans (1) are much more doubtful about climate change than any other nation in the world. Actually, hordes of lobbyists working for the oil and gas industry have been misinforming citizens for decades. Since the US energy independence depended heavily on American oil, underestimating the dangers of its exploitation was but a fair nationalistic argument. Most Republicans were prone to regard scientists as dangerous internationalists, and the Democrats who disagreed with them were, as usual, seen as a communist rabble. Besides, many climate change deniers were mentally unbalanced, which was why they believed that all this was but a conspiracy aimed at protecting the research funding of so-called scientists, or undermining local sovereignty, or making US manufacturing non-competitive, or enabling China to rule the world.

Europeans and Australians are not more intelligent than they, for some of them still believe that climate change does not exist or that there is one that is due to natural factors (2). In France, for instance, although the oil and gas industry does not really try to mislead the general public, in 2022, there were more people who believed that it was caused by natural causes than in 2019. One must admit that there are not so many TV programmes on that matter; there is a growing number of articles on that issue in newspapers, but very few French people get information in that fashion nowadays. Actually, the French distrust scientists, and the COVID-19 period reinforced this feeling; in 2020, 27% of them believed that science is beneficial to humanity. This disbelief is experienced mainly by uneducated people. However, even the French who are not ignoramuses are prone to believe in the nonsense they find on the Web.

That being said, some Westerners are willing to do their best to improve the situation. In fact, Northern Europeans have been limiting their carbon footprint for a long time: cycling and recycling are not novelties in Sweden or the Netherlands. According to an EIB climate survey, many Europeans have already changed their way of life in order to fight climate change. So they eat less red meat, buy local or seasonal products, walk, cycle or use public transport, take the train to go on holiday, heat their houses less in winter, and try not to turn on the air conditioner in summer.

As for the Americans, they are less inclined to adapt to the new situation and advocate temperance. For example, whether they are old or young, they continue to take their cars when they commute or shop. This does not mean that they will not change their minds, for even the inhabitants of Las Vegas – who are not regarded as conservationists – have stopped wasting water. They recycle it, store it, and plant cactuses instead of rose bushes: they are becoming thrifty Swiss Protestants!

Since inaction is no longer possible, in 2015, Westerners and many nations around the world signed the Paris Agreement, whose purpose is to limit the increase in global temperature to 1,5°C. Greenhouse gases emissions should stop by the middle of the 21st century. It is not a treaty but an executive agreement, which means that contracting parties must comply with the regulations, although they have room for manoeuvre. On the 4th of November 2020, the United States, which is the second-largest emitter of greenhouse gases after China, withdrew from the agreement, which showed that some Westerners did not acknowledge the seriousness of the situation. However, on the 20th of January 2020, President Biden signed a document that brought the US back into the Paris Agreement, saying that he wanted to avoid catastrophic planetary warming, which he regarded as a tangible threat.

For the time being, earth's global average surface temperature keeps rising and climate policies are considered to be inadequate. Consequently, some Westerners think that democratic processes do not facilitate radical reforms. This attitude of mind gave birth to a kind of eco-terrorism. In France, ecoterrorists intimidate butchers, throw soup at Mona Lisa (poor dear!), attack the policemen who guard the water reserves which farmers fill in winter so that they may cultivate their fields in summer, and destroy the genetically modified crops. Nevertheless, if they are not democrats, they are not that violent. Similarly, the members of Extinction Rebellion cannot be regarded as dangerous anti-democratic ecoterrorists, for, most of the time, they use nonviolent civil disobedience to compel governments to pass laws that are aimed at protecting the environment. Actually, they use mass arrest to attract attention and to annoy policemen and judges.

We cannot say either that Greta Thunberg, the famous Swedish environmental activist, is a threat to democracy, for she conforms. In 2018, when she began to skip school in order to call for stronger action on climate change, she protested outside the Swedish parliament and therefore acknowledged the legitimacy of its authority, and when she strikes and protest on Fridays, she just behaves in a way that all western democracies consider as legitimate. That being said, it is hard to determine whether her actions are efficient of not. Personally I thing that all those persons keep talking and fussing and that nothing tangible ensues.

B- Some catastrophes to come.

Too little action and willingness led to what we are experiencing today: floods, droughts and wildfires.

Floods, whether they are due to climate change or not, are not major issues, for humans should build buildings where they will be able to withstand heavy rain and its consequences, namely on top of hills, not in valleys where all the water accumulates stubbornly. Hence, when Californian houses are flooded, it is the people who are to blame because they built them where they should have never been built. As to wildfires, one can realize that they are often linked to climate change, for, because of higher temperatures, trees are drier in summer, which is why they catch fire more easily. So, each time there is a heatwave in North America, wildfires consume a growing number of trees.

In June 2021, for instance, during the Pacific Northwest heatwave (4), temperatures reached unprecedented levels in multiple locations. On the 29th of June, Lytton broke Canada's all-time heat record; 49,6°C. is also the highest temperature ever recorded north of 45th parallel north. Much of the city was destroyed by a wildfire. Between the 25th of June (5) and the 2nd of July, 740 excess fatalities were observed in British Columbia. During the heatwave, most deaths occurred in private residences because of high indoor temperatures. In Greater Vancouver, there were more fatalities in neighborhoods with higher material and social deprivation and less parks, and, logically, old people were more affected than the young. In 2023, another heatwave stroke Canada and, once again, exacerbated wildfires. They were so extreme that the smoke reached Minneapolis, New York, and the United Kingdom!

Not only are heatwaves detrimental to humans' health, but also they affect field crops. In British Columbia, in 2021, the wheat crop decreased by 31% and the canola crop by 21% (6). The cranberry bushes were not affected because they are thoroughly watered and the critical growth period happens later in the season. However, in general, all fruit trees that grow well in oceanic and continental climates are affected by global warming. Actually, they need a certain amount of chill hours (below 7,23°C.) in order to break bud dormancy. For instance, a pear tree requires between 500 and 1500 hours, an apple tree between 300 and 1000, and an apricot tree between 600 to 900. When they don't get enough chill hours, trees don't grow well, bloom less and produce less fruit, which is why gardeners have been trying to mitigate the effects of lack of cold for years by creating new hybrids that can withstand climate change (Katy apricot trees and Biloxi blueberries, for example).

Drought is also a serious threat. In California and some parts of the interior of the West (7), droughts are more frequent and last longer. Hence, water restrictions are commonplace, people suffer more from asthma because the soil turns into dust and prevents them from breathing well, and farmers keep emptying aquifers, which caused some areas to sink. This race for groundwater is illusionary, for once aquifers are empty, if farmers don't discover other ways to get water, Californian agriculture will disappear and Americans will have to find other places (in the north) where they will grow their food.

In Europe (8), heatwaves are becoming more frequent and temperatures reach unprecedented levels. To this date, the summer of 2022 was the hottest on record in Europe. In Darnétal (in Normandy), I recorded a temperature that was slightly above 40°C., which is nonsense, for summers are always mild (it is an oceanic climate, not a Mediterranean one). Heatwaves were frequent in Western Europe and the summer was very dry. In France, aquifers were depleted, and they were many water restrictions in the southern localities. Actually, Southern France have been experiencing severe drought for a few years, and the Pyrénées-Orientales region is still in this situation at the beginning of the year 2024, which is not normal.

However, the European country that suffers the most from drought is undoubtedly Spain. More than two-thirds of this country are already concerned by this phenomenon (9), which is why Spaniards are perfectly aware that Spain and the whole world must address this problem thoroughly (10). besides, the east and the south of the country are in a desperate situation. For instance, in the Málaga region, the reservoirs are almost empty, as you can see in the following pictures, but when did the drought started?

The *La Viñuela Reservoir* on the 27th of May 2011 (11).

The *La Viñuela Reservoir* in May 2023 (11).

Most Spanish journalists will answer that it began in 2021, but it really started in 2014, when I recorded that in Cortijo Jacamón (in Iznate, near Málaga) annual precipitation amounted to 43 cm instead of 64 cm. The following years, it did not rain much because of the presence of the Azores High, which prevented the clouds from producing rain. I was always very upset to see massive dark clouds vanish into thin air because of high pressure.

Little by little the La Viñuela Reservoir dried up. In September 2023 (12), the situation was so critical that most municipalities prohibited the use of water for certain hours every day. In the city of Málaga, the water pressure was reduced (13) and they forbade people to water plants, wash cars and fill swimming pools with potable water. Farmers could not keep on watering their fields. Hence, they began to cut their fruit trees (14), all the more so because they lacked reclaimed water. In January 2024, one realizes that drought is irreversible and that most reservoirs are almost empty (15). The situation is so desperate that the authorities are compelled to enlarge the Marbella desalination plant (16), to install mobile ones throughout the province, and to build an expensive big one next to the city of Málaga (17). As a matter of fact, the predictable drought surprised some Westerners, who, although they don't ignore reality, drag their heels on this issue.

Part IV: A besieged fortress.

The Occident is becoming suspicious of the rest of the world because it does not agree with it and sometimes tries to destroy it. Hence, all that does not resemble it is considered as suspect.

Chapter 10: Immigration.

Actually, it worries about immigration, all the more so because there are lots of immigrants in the Occident, and they don't really integrate into western societies.

A- Into the United States.

The United States was created by successive inflows of immigrants, which is what happened to most countries. Nonetheless, most people have forgotten that their forebears were born elsewhere, whereas Americans have not, for that country is not old. In fact, at the end of the 18th century, when the Thirteen Colonies became the United States of America, there were not so many people who lived in that place, which was why immigration was not regarded as a problem; in other words, the country needed workers to develop.

However, not all immigrants were welcome in the US. For example, the 1882 Chinese Exclusion Act and the 1917 Immigration Act prevented Asians from moving to the US. The subsequent regulations aimed to limit immigration from Italy and Eastern Europe: the US had to remain a country composed of white Protestants, namely Germans, English people and Scandinavians. Nevertheless, the 1965 Immigration and Nationality Act abolished the system of national-origin quotas, which changed the demographics of the US: nowadays, most immigrants come from Latin America and Asia. As for the Muslim ones, they have been under scrutiny since the September 11 attacks. In January 2017, President Trump even signed an executive order temporarily suspending entry to the US by persons coming from certain Muslim countries.

That being said, Americans have never disapproved of legal immigration. In 2023 (1), some statisticians compiled a report which showed that American's opinion about this topic has always been quite consistent. For instance, in 2001, 62% of the interviewees declared that immigration was a good thing for the US, in 2013 72% of them agreed on this, and in 2023 68% shared this opinion. In fact, most Americans (53% of the interviewees in 2019) believe that immigrants help the economy by providing low-cost labor; in 1993, 64% of them thought that they hurt the economy by driving wages down. Moreover, they are aware that they take jobs Americans don't want.

Hence, it is little wonder that most interviewees, in 2006 and 2023, are quite or very sympathetic to illegal immigrants. In 2019, 81% of them said that illegal immigrants had to become American citizens if they met certain requirements.

It is believed that unauthorized immigrants account for almost a quarter of the US foreign-born population (2). The number of illegal immigrants in the US remained quite stable (around 10,5 million persons) from 2004 to 2021 (3). One notices that the number of unauthorized immigrants who come from Mexico has decreased sharply. In contrast, in 2021, the countries of origin with the largest unauthorized immigrant populations in the US were El Salvador (800 000 people), India (725 000 people), Guatemala (700 000 people), Honduras (525 000 people), China (375 000 people), and the Dominican Republic (230 000 people). Logically, they settle in states where they can get a low-paid job, which American citizens do not want, namely California, Texas, Florida, New York, New Jersey and Illinois.

In 2023, the Department of Homeland Security (4) stated that authorities had intercepted 3,2 million illegal aliens that year (2,7 million in 2022); those intercepted along the southern border accounted for 76,6% of all illegal immigrants, which proves that, for various reasons, the migratory pressure from Latin America is increasing. Accordingly, since some border towns are overflowing with illegal immigrants, some governors have them conveyed to northern cities like Boston, Chicago and New York (5), which cannot really handle such a situation.

For the time being, Americans are quite puzzled. If 57% of them still believe that immigration is a good thing for the country (6), 60% of them disapprove of President Biden's handling of immigration, although, since October 2023, he has resumed deportation flights to Venezuela (7) and allowed Texas to continue building the border wall that separated the US from Mexico. Ron DeSantis declared that if he were elected president of the United States, he would send the military into Mexico; Donald Trump said that immigrants were "poisoning the blood of our country"; 60% of Republicans (8) think that the government should increase security along the US-Mexico border in order to reduce illegal crossings, whereas only 23% of Democrats agree on that. As a matter of fact, Americans hesitate because they perceive that there is no easy solution, for the world is in disarray.

A family and a man from Latin America crossing in the Tucson Sector of the US-Mexico border (9).

B- Into Europe.

As to Europe, is has become many migrants' destination, which is weird because Europeans left this place for centuries. As a matter of fact, Europe is a finished world in which it's hard to find one's place. Europe is a Pandora's box which nobody should open. In classical antiquity, for instance, the young used to leave Greece and settle down in other parts of the Mediterranean because their fathers' land did not produce enough food for their sons' families. The Greeks were thus doomed to emigrate. When the Spaniards conquered the Americas, a great meany Andalusians and inhabitants of Extremadura were happy to flee poverty and take a chance on the New World. As for the English who immigrated to the Thirteen Colonies, most of them also wanted to lead a better life in what was regarded as a land of opportunity.

The migration of Europeans accelerated in the 19th and at the beginning of the 20th century because governments were unable to address important issues such as famine, revolutions, wars, mechanization, class struggle and demographic transition; they mostly went to the United States. Hence, there were very few immigrants and non-Europeans in Europe, although some European countries possessed colonies in different parts of the world. Actually, colonized peoples were not supposed to live in the mother country. Nevertheless, during World War I, indigenous people served in the European armed forces, and, after the war, a few Black Americans (like Josephine Baker) fleeing racial segregation moved to Europe.

After, the Second World War, European economy and society were in ruins. Since there were not enough Europeans to rebuild what had been destroyed, European nations systematized immigration from their colonies, and decolonization did not stop the process. Consequently, millions of Africans settled down in Northern Europe and became the workers who built the schools, roads, houses and stores that enabled this place to overcome the aftermath of World War II and thrive. However, because of several economic crises, certain governments tried to slow immigration, but they were unsuccessful because Africans and Asians still believe that their lives will be better if they immigrate to Europe.

In fact, there is a growing number of people who migrate (10), for there are more people on the planet and more political and social problems in certain parts of the world. Consequently, the proportion of foreigners in the European population is rising. The wars in Syria and Ukraine, a high rate of unemployment in Northern Africa, social and political problems in the Middle East, and the explosion of the population in the center and the south of Africa aggravated the situation. Europe is overflowing with refugees, who reach it by crossing the Sahara or the Mediterranean Sea, which has become a graveyard. They besiege Melilla and Ceuta or board small boats in order to reach Lampedusa or Greece; they hide in the trucks that pass through the Channel Tunnel and wander around Europe in the hope of being accepted as political refugees and getting asylum in any European country.

This migration crisis worsened between 2007 and 2011, which moved the Greeks and the Bulgarians to erect a fence along the Turkish border. Thousands of migrants drowned in the Mediterranean as they tried to cross it. On the 2nd of September 2015, the dead bodies of Alan Kurdi (aged 3), his brother (aged 5) and his mother (aged 27) were found lying on a Turkish beach; Europeans' indifference to the plight of all migrants impelled them to shed crocodile tears. On the 22nd of September 2015, the interior ministers of the countries that belong to the European Union decided to stop immigration (which is illegal!) and to allow the asylum seekers who were in Greece and Italy to go and stay in other European countries. However, the influx of refugees did not stop. In 2023 (11), there was a sharp rise in illegal border crossings, which amounted to 380 000. Syrians accounted for 26% of illegal immigrants. Actually Syrian, Guineans and Afghans account for 37% of illegal immigrants, who are mostly men.

Migrants rescued by the Spanish NGO Open Arms near Lampedusa on the 3rd of August 2023 (12).

At first, the German government agreed to take charge of many refugees in order to support Germany's economy. Actually, German women do not have enough children, which causes the population to grow old. Hence, German society needs young people because they can have and raise children as they take care of the elderly and get the jobs which Germans cannot assume or don't want. In 2015, there were so many immigrants and many European governments were so annoyed by the Germans' point of view that the German government restored the border between Germany and Austria in order to stop the influx of refugees. On New Year's Eve 2015, some male refugees described as Arabs or North Africans sexually assaulted women in Cologne, which moved the Prime Minister to facilitate the deportation of such criminals. Besides, statistics (13) show that those foreigners have difficulty getting a job and that they don't easily integrate into European society because they don't speak European languages very well and are uneducated.

On the other hand, Europeans were shocked by the violence they exhibited. The German authorities had to admit that migrants had committed many crimes, that some of them had been involved in the 2016 Berlin truck attack and that Germans used to take revenge on them, which added to public disorder and to the feeling that the state was losing control. Similarly, the French and Belgian authorities declared that some of the terrorists who were involved in the November 2015 Paris attacks and the 2016 Brussels bombings had crossed the EU borders pretending that they were refugees, which tarnished a bit more their reputation and turned them into dangerous criminals from whom Europeans had to protect themselves.

Chapter 11: Islamic terrorism.

On the morning of the 11th of September 2001, when an airplane crashed into the north face of the World Trade Center's North Tower, all Westerners were puzzled. When other planes crashed into the South Tower's southern facade, the west side of the Pentagon, and a field near Shanksville, in Pennsylvania, they realized that it was a terrorist attack. Later on, when the plot was revealed, they wondered whether this was the beginning of a conflict between Islam and the Occident, a kind of clash of civilizations.

A- In the United States.

Bear in mind that neither the US nor the other western countries have always been hated by Muslims. In fact, after World War II, excepting the nations that had been defeated by them, most people regarded the Americans as people who had been able to keep things in perspective, collaborate with Russians and end a war that resembled the end of the world. Besides, even if Muslims had often considered that Westerners were but cruel crusaders, they did not hate them to the extent that they wanted to exterminate them all. Actually, in the Islamic community, Americans' reputation began to deteriorate when they backed the Israeli government, which systematically colonized the Palestinian territories as it systematically bullied Muslim citizens. The Iran hostage crisis, in 1979, when 52 American diplomats and citizens were held hostage by Iranian student who supported the Iranian Revolution, added fuel to the fire. Ayatollah Ruhollah Musavi Khomeini, the supreme leader of Iran from 1979 to 1989, thought that the US was an imperialist power that was corrupting the whole world and which he named the Great Satan. Then various military interventions in the Middle East turned the US into a genuine nuisance.

Osama bin Laden, head of al Qaeda and one of the persons who orchestrated the September 11 attacks, opined on the Americans. It is clear that he hated them and that his hatred of them was linked to the US government's policy towards the Islamic world. In 1996, in his first Fatwa (1), he charged the Americans with perpetrating atrocities against Muslims and with forming an alliance with the Jews (which he called the Jewish-Christian alliance) in order to expel the Muslims from Palestine. In his second fatwa (2), he demonized them and compared them with locusts that swarm around Muslims' riches and eat them. In his 2002 (3) letter to the Americans, he was more specific about the Jewish-Christian alliance. He declared that it had attacked the Muslims in Palestine, whom he regarded as true Semites and thus as the inheritors of Moses. Then he listed the nations that had been persecuted by the Americans and told them that they had to convert to Islam, which was the only way to repent and redeem themselves. He added that they had to stop supporting Israel and had to leave the Middle East. But what kind of personality did Osama bin Laden have?

First of all, his ego was weak. In 1999, Rachimullah Jusufzai described him as courteous, soft-spoken, shy and unassuming (4), and when we analyse what he said in the interviews, we realize that he considered that any trace of hostility towards him attacked his self-esteem, which he wanted to protect by being reserved. This man hated aggressive people. In a 1996 interview (5), he described a young mujaheddin named Al-Tahir and emphasized his intelligence and politeness. He feared the judgment of others and the way they behaved and looked at him. Eye contact was a serious matter, and people who did not follow decorum were deemed rude and dangerous. Politeness was a modus vivendi and a modus operandi, which proves that he was not a psychopath, since he behaved himself. It also demonstrates that he did not interact well with most people: clumsy statements and bad manners harmed his narcissism.

He was so touchy that he considered that the presence of the Americans in Saudi Arabia, during and after the Gulf War, was an insult (6). That same year, he declared that the opponents (like him) of the Saudi regime had been ridiculed and humiliated (7); intellectuals were also ridiculed by the king (8); he came to the conclusion that "Death is better than life in humiliation and shame" (9). Some months later, the Saudi regime was regarded as arrogant (10), whereas, in Yemen, the air was "unblemished with humiliation" (11). He added that, in order to tarnish his reputation, some governments were spreading rumors that he wanted to live in the United Kingdom (12). In 1999, he asked the Americans (13) to choose a better government, which would not blemish the reputation of the other nations. In 2002, he warned them about their crusade against the Muslims and told them that, as usual, they would end up being humiliated by the mujaheddin (14).

On the other hand, he used Islam as a psychological crutch. He did not have individual conscience, and, of course, he was not an original thinker. The absence of some essential concepts compelled him to follow the preconceived ideas of others. Hence, Islam enabled him to interact, for if it did not enlighten him about all issues, at least it clarified many daily life problems. James Pennebaker and Cindy Chung (15) analyzed the data by means of a computer, and they concluded that Bin Laden used to think in a more complicated way than Zawahiri. This does not mean that he was intelligent; it is just being between the devil and the deep blue sea! He kept quoting from the Quran, which shows that religion helped him to think. A man with a neurotic personality usually quotes his parents, especially his father (for his morals form part of his son's superego). He was unable to do so because his father, who died when he was ten, did not really raise him. The sacred book had replaced the paternal superego. So he would obey father surrogates like Muhammad and God; he stated (16): "Allah is the one who provides guidance". These father figures were dangerous, for they were linked to omnipotence: the individual had to obey or die.

Sacred books do not explain; sometimes readers misinterpret what is written, which leads to manslaughter.

Thanks to Allah, he avoided sin. Although he did not know what morality was, he knew what immorality was since the Quran provided the answer. Consequently, polytheism, sorcery, usury, taking the money of orphans, alcohol, adultery, disobeying parents, perjury, slandering innocent, faithful women, fleeing combat, and murder (unless God permits it) were regarded as sins. Moreover, Bin Laden reinterpreted the Islamic concepts and expressed his opinions. For instance, when he referred to Bill Clinton's affair with Monica Lewinsky, he was aware that he had committed adultery and that he should have been punished, but he also provided a piece of information which Muhammad did not know: he said that the sexual sins committed by the Americans enabled AIDS to spread across the world, especially across poor countries. This remark shows that Bin Laden considered that sexuality was a problem since his subconscious did not prevent him from saying in an interview what a person with a neurotic personality might have concealed.

As for his opinion about war, it is devoid of morality. When people were killed by mujaheddin, he did not feel any sorrow (17). He even agreed to kill (18), which proves that his desire for murder was a key component of his personality and that he was amoral. Actually, he did not mind being called a murderer (19). For instance, when he described the Americans' occupation of the Grand Mosque during the Gulf war, he misinterpreted reality since the Americans, who had been invited by King Fahd, never occupied it, nor did they occupy Saudi Arabia! However, he declared that the Americans and the Jews had to be expelled and that history would decide whether he is a criminal or not.

Even when he speaks of the Palestinians, one doubts his sincerity, for his arguments are specious and may mean something else. In fact, when he spoke of the Palestine Liberation Organization and of the

Palestinian authority, he stated (20) that they sympathized with the infidels. He did not say that they were traitors, but he emphasized that they had not achieved any goal because they were not violent. When the journalist told him that many Muslims disapproved of violence, he answered that fighting was a part of Islam. So people who did not fight were sinners.

Feeling harassed was one of his personality traits. The harassers were the Jews and, above all, the Americans: he kept bashing them. This hatred had turned the shy, well-mannered man into a restless, talkative extremist. The wars in Palestine and Lebanon served as a pretext for feeling endangered by nonbelievers. Any attack on Sunnis was viewed as violence against him: the incomplete psychological identification did not enable him to differentiate between him and people whom he believed to be like him (21). Even though he spent much of his life outside Saudi Arabia, he remained an Arab: he kept talking about the corrupted regime, the wicked princes, and the arrogant king. He regarded Mecca as a kind of lighthouse, but why?

Actually, the most sacred mosques of the Arab World were so damaged that they had to be restored or even rebuilt: Osama Bin Laden's father, who was a well-known building contractor, had been asked to repair the Dome of the Rock, in Jerusalem, and to rebuild the Prophet's Mosque, in Medina, and the Grand Mosque, in Mecca, which he did. The places which the Muslims regarded as the holiest shrines meant a lot to the little Osama, who did not know his father well but admired him. According to him, this mission had been ordered by God and, to a certain extent, sanctified by him (22). He rarely spoke of his father, but when he did, he was not a grown man recalling the good moments spent with him but a believer speaking of a Saint who deserved the best place in heaven. Consequently, when the Jews and the Christians were too close to the monuments rebuilt by his father, he panicked and almost behaved like a psychotic. In fact, he displayed paranoid traits when he spoke of the United States. In 1996

(23), he had already declared that a conspiracy had been organized by the Americans and their allies, but he had not said which goal they wanted to achieve. He enumerated wars in which the Americans were supposed to take part, but this so-called plot was but a flight of fancy. In 2001 (24), the conspiracy began to take shape: according to him, the Americans wanted to conquer Saudi Arabia and the Grand Mosque. Hence, the plan had been hatched by the Christians and Bush was undoubtedly the most dangerous crusader. His idea of Christianity was so fuzzy that American Protestants became Catholic crusaders!

As for Mohamed Atta, he hijacked American Airlines Flight 11, which crashed into the North Tower of the World Trade Center.

In 2012, Adam Lankford had a very good idea (25): he reclassified terrorists as "lunatics". Actually, he gathered information about Mohamed Atta and noticed that he was suicidal. Psychiatrists and psychologists are puzzled by suicide, all the more so because Freud never really studied it. Besides, depression is not a manifestation they fully understand; they use this word when they describe the mood of an obsessive, or a schizophrenic, or a psychopath, and they rarely dare to attribute it to a psychosis called melancholy, which could be placed between paranoia and schizophrenia. Adam Lankford was thorougher than they. Moreover, he knew that suicide is not an Islamic custom, and he put great emphasis on Atta's idiosyncrasies, which moved him to regard depression as a symptom of madness.

Personally, I was intrigued by his 1996 will (26), for he described how he wanted his body to be treated, although, after a suicide attack (he was planning one), the Muslim funeral rites cannot be performed, and they are not necessary. Actually, this will is rather absurd, but let's analyse it carefully.

The first oddity is his abhorrence of women, which transcends death. Once dead, sex is not a problem anymore. Since he is an immature person, his fear is intense; he wrote (27): "I don't want a pregnant woman or a person who is not clean to come and say good-bye to me...". He rejects women not because they can give birth but because they are unclean when they are pregnant. He fears that he is going to be infected, which might be a symptom of severe depression, but he adds that there will be no women during the burial, and he forbids them to visit his grave. Being a pregnant woman is defilement, and being a woman is an abomination. He does not stand them, even in the afterlife. However, this strange gender threat is also caused by men! He declares that the man who will wash his body will have to wear gloves because he does not want a man to touch his genitals without a kind of protective shield. Sex petrified him. This castration anxiety suppresses the libido. We must not only blame his father, for he was so close to his mother that she must also be responsible for this personality disorder.

The second oddity is the parable of the ashes; he wrote (28): "You should throw the dust on my body three times while saying from the dust, we created you from dust and to dust you will return. From the dust a new person will be created. ...". The first assertion is quite common, the second one is not; it shows that he believed that he would be resurrected from the dead and that he would be transformed certainly into a more perfect man. I suspect he did not like himself very much; I also suspect he believed that there was something wrong with his body and his mind maybe. The caterpillar wanted to become a butterfly; a bad womb had borne a bad son, and only God could remake him through death.

Of course, suicide is forbidden by religion since Hell is the final destination of a Muslim who kills himself in this fashion. Hence, suicidal Muslims are bound for martyrdom. Muslim societies mitigate the population's desire for murder in this way since it is directed towards the outside of the Muslim world, which may protect the sane part of society. Nevertheless, when those persons lose touch with reality, this tactic can backfire.

As for Mohamed Atta, his suicidal behaviour depended on the eternal enemy: the United States. He wanted to die; since he did not get a medical treatment, he was bound to kill himself in a suicide attack. The information does not allow us to discern the psychological process that led him to plan the September 11 attacks and to choose to crash a plane into the North Tower (World Trade Center). Adam Lankford depicts him as a loner who was impressed by the pilgrimage he made to Mecca in 1995. After this date, he could identify his arch-enemy: once again, the Jews were regarded as devilish plotters. When he was in Hamburg, he became more antisocial: his roommates could hardly stand him. He was aware that they hated him; at least once he asked an acquaintance of his why he did not like him. Here we can only hypothesize that he was more unstable after his pilgrimage, which moved him to find an ultimate solution: he wrote his will in 1996 because he wanted to carry out a suicide attack, which he finally did five years later. Although Al Qaeda's global jihadism enabled us to see two very immature persons act, we cannot identify a trend, which is why me must study what happened in France in 2015 and 2016.

B- In France.

The terrorist attacks that took place in France in 2015 and 2016 horrified and perplexed the general public because a great many persons were killed. Authorities wondered why a perfect democracy that enabled citizens to be free and happy could be hated by youngsters, criminologists wondered whether certain circumstances had created such monsters, and psychologists wondered whether they were sane or insane.

Actually, Nicolas Campel and his colleagues examined the research papers that dealt with Islamic radicalization and noticed that specialists had put great emphasis on theses youths' psychological vulnerability.

According to them, radicalized youths were often depressed, had experienced abandonment, had grown up without a father, and had mothers who had been unable to raise them properly because they were depressed, or suicidal, or disabled (29). Then Nicolas Campel and his colleagues examined data about 150 young radicalized individuals surveilled by the police in order to discover trends and perhaps confirm that those persons had at least a personality disorder (30).

The average age of the young French radicalized Muslims they surveyed was around 20 years; 67% were females and 33% males. 34% of them were of North African or Middle Eastern descent, which is not a lot. 29,3% of them used to self-harm or were suicidal, 35,3% had already consulted a psychiatrist, 44% had exhibited symptoms of depression, 60% had had an overly close relationship with a relative, 82% had experienced abandonment, 85% had been mentally abused or neglected, and 40,7% had a mother who suffered from depression. In short, most of them were emotionally unstable, that is, immature persons whose mode of decompensation is nervous breakdown, which makes sense when we compare their cases to those of Khaled Kelkal and Mohamed Merah, who are, in a way, typical French Jihadists.

Khaled Kelkal epitomizes the post-colonial Algerian immigration. He was born in Mostaganem (Algeria) in 1971 and settled in Vaulx-en-Velin, near Lyon, in 1973. According to him (31), he behaved himself when he attended primary school. He began committing larceny when he attended junior high school and became a professional thief some years later. In 1990 (he was 19), he was already sentenced to six months in prison. On the 26th of August 1995, after some terrorist attacks in France, the police found his fingerprints on the adhesive tape that covered a home-made bomb. On the 29th of September 1995, he was killed by the police; he was 24. Fortunately, two years before his death, a sociologist had interviewed him. This interview was published after Kelkal's death; it gives us valuable information about his mind.

When we read Dietmar Loch's printed interview, we notice Kelkal's "suburban way of speaking", which is a kind of degraded French. For instance, he forgot the double negatives, had difficulty conjugating verbs (he had issues with the subjunctive), and chose words that did not mean exactly what he wanted to say. Maybe French was not his mother tongue, but he was also unable to speak Arabic (he learned it in prison). In fact, French was the only language he could speak, although he was not fluent in it. His vocabulary did not contain words that came from the local patois (32), which proves that Kelkal's French had nothing to do with his neighbor's culture; it was the language of the youngsters who neither want adults to understand them nor want to resemble them. His vocabulary showed that he was immature, especially when he spoke about his school, which her regarded as a fun place.

Of course, he displayed symptoms of borderline personality disorder. For instance, when he spoke of his life before his stay in prison, he described himself as impulsive and violent. His definition of robbery was even more meaningful: according to him, stealing was similar to being free and playing a game. In fact, the juvenile delinquent derives pleasure from the possibility that he could fail. If he doesn't, he feels as if he were stronger than the others, and he deceives the victim and the police, who represent the superego he does not really have.

Besides, his ego is weak, he has low self-esteem, and he belongs to an anaclitic group, which led him to formulate the concept of "unicity". According to him, it means that people look alike and interact socially, which is the definition of unity. He was quite immoral. At the end of the interview, he admitted that people had to follow rules, but he also declared that, when he was in high school, he was unprincipled; he added that he was not really able to understand what goodness was.

His religious faith may be connected to the construction of his superego. We do not know when he began to go to the Mosque and whether his father taught him the basics of Islam. Nonetheless, he declared that when he was in junior high school he used to pray, and therefore he did not have any vice and felt good and balanced. The day when he stopped praying, he got into trouble and went to jail. Hence, although his superego was quite inoperative, he had a notion of goodness and he was aware that people had to be righteous so that they might live a harmonious life without getting into trouble. This proves that he was not that immature.

Islam was also the path to what he perceived as his country: Algeria. When he was in jail, a Muslim inmate who was fluent in Arabic taught him this tongue. We do not know whether he studied divinity, but he declared that he used to watch videos showing Muslim scholars. God and religion gave meaning to his life, they clarified everything in the universe, and they put his chaotic world in order, which enabled him to build his life and identify with human beings who were Muslims; he wrote (33): "... I am neither Arab nor French: I am a Muslim. ... Whether you are Asiatic, or Black, or Red, it does not matter because if you are a Muslim, we are brothers. ...". The role models he did not find in his family, he found them in Islam.

However, he was not mature enough not to carry out the 1995 terrorist attacks, though he was not a brainless psychopath who wanted to kill everybody.

As for Mohamed Merah, his psychological evaluation had been performed in 2009 (he was 20) by Alain Pénin: he had already had issues with the police, and the judge had ordered psychologists to examine him in order to adapt the sentence (34).

Alain Pénin met him at the Seyne penitentiary on the 15th of January 2009. He pointed out that he was nervous and that he took sleeping pills and psychotropics in order to calm his anxiety. He had formerly tried to hang himself. He stayed in a psychiatric hospital from the 25th of December 2008 to the 8th of January 2009. This psychologist wrote that he was in tune with reality, that what he said was logical, and that his brain's processing speed was high, but he had difficulty with abstract thinking. The tests (including the Rorschach test) showed that he perceived reality as it was, which implies that he had gone through the process of psychological identification. However, the image of his mother caused him anxiety. He declared that he was quiet and liked being alone. He used to spruce himself up, but he did not flirt with girls. He was depressed and suicidal. He enjoyed reading the Quran and praying; he observed Ramadan. He neither drank alcohol, nor took drugs, nor smoke. He had committed antisocial acts and had difficulty learning from experience. Alain Pénin stated that he was an emotionally immature individual. According to him, the tests showed that he had resolved the Oedipus complex and that his personality was unstable, which is a psychoanalytic incongruity since this individual's personality was not organized at the neurotic level (35). I must add that he did not speak French very well: I noticed some misspellings and his vocabulary was limited. This psychologist realized that Merah was an immature man, but one must refute the assumptions he made about Merah's quietness and about the resolution of the Oedipus complex.

If this psychological evaluation is not excellent, Doria's documentary is irreplaceable (36), for it enables us to understand who Merah was and to determine, to a certain extent, the factors which shaped his personality.

It is self-evident that he is the product of a dysfunctional family: his mother reproached herself for having divorced his father and declared that she was unable to raise her five children because no man helped her. That being said, her husband was not a good role model: he was a drug dealer and was sentenced to five years in prison. Hence, no man separated Mohamed from his mother, or inculcated moral values in him, or helped him to interact with people, which is why he did whatever he liked. His mother was so overwhelmed that she contacted the social services. He was sent to an institution, and a document dated August 18, 1997 (he was nine) shows that, at home, the situation was problematic.

When he was fourteen, he was very aggressive: he kept insulting girls, stealing, destroying goods and assaulting people. He refused to comply with requests from adults: he was the typical psychopath. His mother stated that at an unspecified age he told her several times that there were two persons in his head. Is it a dissociative identity disorder, delusion of being controlled, or a hallucination? It is impossible to answer, but one must assume that his personality had been prearranged at the psychotic level. If after the end of the Oedipus complex he did not become a psychotic, he failed to become a person with a neurotic personality. However, he was mentally unbalanced.

At the age of sixteen, he became a bit more sociable. He already led a double life: during the day he worked in a garage and showed that he was reliable, at night he stole cars and committed robberies. On the 18th of December 2007 he was sentenced to 18 months in prison. He went to jail for the first time, and it was a traumatic experience. We do not know exactly why, but one can assume that the other inmates bullied him, which unsettled him and ruined his self-esteem. After one year in prison, he made a rope out of bed sheets and tried to hang himself.

Then he was released. He could further his education by visiting Muslim websites. In July 2010, he went to Syria in order to meet some mujaheddin. In Islamabad, in the summer of 2011, he met Abdul Aziz Gazi, an imam who knew Bin Laden, and attended a terrorist training camp near Miranshah, in Pakistan.

On the 11th of March 2012 around 8 O'clock in the morning, in a school, he killed three young children (aged 4, 5 and 7) and a teacher: they were Jewish. The days before, he had killed three soldiers: two of them were Muslims! He declared that he wanted to kill soldiers because they had taken part in the Afghanistan War and used to kill Muslims. In a letter found in his bag, he wrote that he was an Al Qaeda soldier who fought for the sake of his Afghan brothers, but why did he kill children? In fact, he did not care about religion since he killed

Muslims! Did he want to kill Jews? No, he wanted to kill children and regress to primitive omnipotence, which is characterized by oral sadism. He was so suicidal that he said to the police: "I let it be known that the man who faces you does not fear death. I like it as much as you like life." Then he did not express regret; he just said that he would have liked to kill more soldiers and children.

On the 7th of January 2015, Saïd and Chérif Kouachi burst into the meeting room of the satirical newspaper Charlie Hebdo and shot eight journalists down because they used to mock and belittle Muslims. Unfortunately, the police killed the two attackers, which does not allow us to get much information about their attitude of mind. However, on the 15th of January 2015 (37), Eloïse Lebourg, a journalist, published a paper which shows that theses murderers could not have been sane people, for they had not known their father, they had been raised by a mother who did not take care of them, they had been probably traumatized by her death, they might have been bullied by some of the inhabitants of the violent neighborhood in which they lived, and they had been sent to an orphanage. In contrast, Amédy Coulibaly, an acquaintance of theirs, who, at the same moment, killed a policewoman in Montrouge and four persons who were shopping at a Jewish supermarket in Vincennes, had been examined by psychiatrists after he had been arrested by the police, in 2010, because they believed that he had helped Aït Ali Belkacem (a famous French Islamic terrorist) to escape from prison. A psychiatrist had declared that Coulibaly was not a lunatic but an "immature person and a psychopath". A psychologist had noticed that he was immoral and not self-aware, that he hardly knew why he acted, and that he had illusions of omnipotence.

On the 14th of July 2016, Mohamed Lahouaiej-Bouhlel, a Tunisian citizen who lived in France and was married to a cousin of his, who was French, ran over people who had just watched the Bastille Day firework and killed 86 of them. Depending on observers' intelligence, he was regarded either as a normal guy or a raving maniac! Chamseddine Hamouda (38), the psychiatrist who had examined him on the 20th of August 2004, thought that he was on the verge of lunacy, for he had difficulty establishing the limits of his own body, he was violent, and he kept to himself. So he had prescribed Haldol (an antipsychotic), Tranxene (a tranquilizer) and Elavil (an antidepressant). He did not want to see the psychiatrist again because the medication made him sleep, which prevented him from understanding what the professors said in class (39). In October 2022, during the trial, his ex-wife told the judges that on two occasions he had tried to kill himself. His father declared that he was a drunkard. Mohamed was so violent that his father used to beat him. He even compelled him to live alone in a small apartment when he was 16 or 17. Both agreed on the fact that he had gone crazy when he had killed all those persons.

Later on, when he moved to Nice, he was described as a loner, a weirdo and a villain, who used to eat pork, drink alcohol, take drugs, mistreat his wife, break the law, date a great many persons, and be violent (40).

The least I can say is that this man was unbalanced. Nonetheless, I feel certain that he was not a psychotic, for nobody asserted that he used to experience hallucinations. Besides, all the symptoms that have been described can be attributed to very immature individuals who are losing touch with reality because they are getting very depressed.

Hence, all the so-called jihadists we have just examined were far from being sane, but they were not insane either.

Chapter 12: Nationalism.

It is clear that Westerners are disturbed by mass migration, all the more so because immigrants' religious and political believes seem to conflict with theirs. Besides, the Occident is so intolerant of disagreement that it dreams of brainwashing them into believing that they have always been strong advocates of democracy, Christianity and capitalism.

A- In the north of Europe.

Some Westerners are more intolerant than others. Bear in mind that Europeans rarely accept people who don't resemble them. Not so long ago, some of them even tried to exterminate a whole race in Poland; not so long ago, the Serbians intended to exterminate Bosnians and Croatians. Europeans boast that they actively promote human rights, but it is they who committed the first crimes against humanity. Hence, it is little wonder that nationalism based on racial hatred is on the rise in the north of Europe.

In Norway, Islam is the biggest religious minority, and Statistics Norway estimates that around 200 000 inhabitants are Muslims, which accounts for 4% of the population. In a survey conducted in 2017 (1), 42% of the interviewees said that Muslims did not want to integrate into Norwegian society and 31% declared that they wanted to take over Europe. As a matter of fact, Norwegians view Islam as an antiquated oddity, a religion that moves worshipers to be violent fanatics. They regard Muslims as social misfits who hate democracy, mistreat women, take advantage of the system, and pose a threat to the nation.

Actually, history tells us that Norwegian governments used to implement policies aimed at uniformizing society, which was why they compelled the Sámi to integrate. The state wanted to create a nation that was racially, religiously, linguistically and culturally homogeneous. As timed passed, the influx of immigrants (including the Poles and the Swedes) turned Norwegian society into a multicultural one (2). Since in democracies any kind of discontent influences political parties, the *Progress Party* integrated immigration issues into its manifesto. In brief, the party wants to restrict immigration to "good refugees", namely those who are educated and righteous and comply with western values such as tolerance, freedom of speech and democracy. Consequently, its members disapprove of illegal immigration because they want to protect Norway from dangerous aliens. Honestly, one cannot regard them as right-wing extremists, for the nationalism they advocate is at an embryonic stage.

In Denmark, too, there is a growing feeling of fear of foreign-born persons, who are seen as dangerous people who do not want to integrate into Danish society, which moves certain Danes to vote for parties that advocate border control in order to protect this people and its national identity. There, too, the smallest acts aimed at helping people who don't come from the same background or don't have the same religion as the natives of Denmark to coexist with them are greatly exaggerated, which shocks the general public (3). Danish society appears a besieged fortress that wants to protect its whiteness from any trace of foreign impurity.

Founded in 1995, the *Danish People's Party* unites the Danes who want to protect themselves from an arch-enemy whose identity is no secret: Islam. The party leaders reject multiculturalism and thus immigration since it dilutes Danish identity. They would like to reduce migrations flows from non-western countries and force the non-Westerners who dwell in Denmark to assimilate. They are so Islamophobic that they supported the Danish government's participation in the military operation launched by the French in Mali (which was aimed at defeating Islamist factions) and systematically oppose Turkey's plan for joining the European Union. They feel so insecure that they are suspicious of the EU and don't want to adopt the euro.

As for the Swedes, who are usually less fearful and much more open-minded than the other Scandinavians, they are also tempted to withdraw into themselves, which takes the form of nationalism.

The party called *The Sweden Democrats* was founded in 1988. Back then, it was disregarded because of its neo-Nazi tendencies (4). As time went by, waves of immigration turned certain areas like Malmö into multi-ethnic places where violence reigned: statistics (5) show that more crimes are committed in such neighborhoods. Besides, certain riots (for instance, in Malmö in 2008 and in Stockholm in 2013) led many Swedes to believe that if non-Westerners were not always dangerous persons, they were at least a danger to public order and the way of life of Westerners. Actually, the inflection point was the 2015 European Refugee Crisis. The influx of immigrant was so massive that the Social Democrat Prime Minister declared that the Swedish government could not handle the situation well. Consequently, the Swedes began to vote for *The Sweden Democrats*: in the 2010 general elections, 5,7% of electors voted for them, which enabled them to enter the Swedish parliament for the first time, and in 2022, 20,6% of electors voted for them, which allowed them to assume the chairmanship of four parliamentary committees.

Their ideology is characterized by the rejection of Islam. For instance, in 2009, Jimmie Akesson, the leader of *The Sweden Democrats*, declared that Islam and the Muslims who resided in Sweden were a major threat, for he believed that they wanted to implement the Sharia, that the rape rate would increase because Muslim men are used to raping women, and that some swimming clubs would introduce separate timetables for men and women. Muslims are seen as the arch-enemies of the Swedes, which leads them to withdraw into themselves. This behavior is almost pathological since party members tend to view any foreigner as a threat, which is why they oppose free movement of workers in the EU and want to restrict temporary work visas so that only the foreigners who take the jobs which Swedish citizens don't want may be allowed to stay in the country. In contrast, Scandinavian workers would be allowed to dwell in Sweden and take any kind of job. Besides, they are Eurosceptic, want to keep their currency, are against Turkey's accession to the EU, and threaten to leave the EU if it became a confederation like the USA. Actually, they would like to form an alliance with the other Nordic countries in order to create a kind of Lebensraum populated by people who belong to the same ethnic group and come from the same background.

B- In the south and the west of Europe.

In the south and the west of Europe, nationalism is gaining ground too.

Spain has a long tradition of authoritarian regimes. When the duke of Anjou became king of Spain in 1700, copying his grand-father Louis XIV, he tried to centralize the state and to unify a country that was but a juxtaposition of regions in which the inhabitants wanted to preserve local customs and their languages. In the 19th century, the sovereign did not really govern the country; it was the prime minister's duty, who was often a serviceman, for it was understood that this kind of person was able to maintain law and order. So, when Francisco Franco seized power, in 1936, and established a dictatorship, it was neither surprising nor unusual.

Franco died in 1975 and the regime ended in 1978. In 1981, Antonio Tejero executed a coup d'état, which failed. Were Spaniards nostalgic for Fascism? I doubt it, for when I lived in Spain, I rarely met people who said that life was better when Franco was alive. I only read once a graffito, in Malaga, which said that retirees were wealthier back then and that democracy did not bring wealth to the country. Actually, there is no real nostalgia for that regime because Franco died a long time ago. Consequently, contemporary Spanish nationalism cannot be regarded as an attempt to re-establish a centralizing authoritarian regime in Spain. Nevertheless, there is a political organization that can be regarded as a far-right party and which is very antagonistic towards Islam and advocates centralization: *Vox*. It was founded in 2013 in order to defend the Spanish nation against its enemies, especially the Muslims.

Santiago Abascal (7)

Santiago Abascal, its leader, is profoundly Islamophobic and hostile to immigration, although, in 2019 (8), he declared that if Spain needed immigrants, they would have to be Latin Americans because they speak Spanish and come from almost the same background as Spaniards. In July 2023 (9), he published the manifesto of the party, in which he stated that he wanted the Navy to patrol the coasts of Spain in order to prevent all migrants from reaching the country. If illegal immigrants were caught, they would immediately be deported to their countries, even if they were children. In October 2023 (10), he said that illegal immigration was connected with terrorism and that he had asked the members of his party who belonged to regional governments to refuse to house the 13 000 immigrants who had arrived in the Canary Islands in 2023.

As for Italian nationalists, they are much more influenced by classical fascism than Spaniards. Giorgia Meloni herself, the Prime Minister of Italy since October 2022 and co-founder of *Brothers of Italy*, is the ex-leader of the *National Alliance*, which is a post-fascist party. Bear in mind that the political unification of Italy was a difficult process. In fact, after the fall of the Roman Empire, this place was a juxtaposition of city-states and small principalities that fought one another for centuries. Parochialism prevented Italians from seeing their neighbors as non-enemies. When Napoleon conquered this place, they began to realize that a centralized state could enable them to coexist peacefully. The subsequent political unification of Italy (from 1848 to 1871) reconnected them with the logic of the Roman Empire: an emperor maintains order by means of a centralized state that moderates particularisms. In this regard, Benito Mussolini was but a kind of Roman emperor. Besides, the Italian Republic was unable to defeat the arch-enemy of peace: the Mafia. Hence, a great many Italians (11) consider that Italian fascism is much different to Nazism and that it is not evil incarnate.

Furthermore, the party's ideology is very conventional. Giorgia Meloni herself is a Roman Catholic who defends the nation and the nuclear family.

Giorgia Meloni (12)

Hence, she opposes same-sex marriage and immigration, which is logical. Since Lampedusa is repeatedly invaded by hordes of illegal immigrants, which disrupts society and the state, one realizes that the Italian government needs help so that it may address this issue.

As to contemporary French nationalism, it was influenced by the Second World War since some of the first leaders and members of the *National Front* had supported Marshal Pétain, who had entered into agreement with the Nazis and thus agreed to deport thousands of Jews, who were exterminated in concentration camps in Poland. However, at the beginning, the Front National was not just a gathering of the

French Nazis who had collaborated with the Germans. Actually, this party was very much influenced by the Algerian War, which led its members to loathe the Muslims, who had deprived the French of a part of the Empire. The new arch-enemies of France were undoubtedly the Muslims who lived in Northern Africa. Hence, this party's hatred of Islam is much more ancient than that of the above-mentioned political parties. However, it worsened after the 9/11 and the November 2015 Paris attacks. That being said, in general, party members oppose immigration because they want the natives of France to be better treated than foreigners: it is they who must get a job, a council home and help.

As time went by, French society had to address more and more issues, and the French began to vote for the *National Front*. In 2002, Jean-Marie Le Pen succeeded in going into the second round of the presidential election, which appalled the other Europeans. In 2017 and 2022, his daughter Marine Le Pen achieved the same goal, and the same year, 89 party members joined the French National Assembly. They formed the largest group of political opponents. Actually, this party is lying in ambush. Marine Le Pen, Jordan Bardella and many supporters strive hard to be regarded as ordinary people in order to come into power.

Hence, global disorder, terrorism and mass migration revived old utopias, which are a survival strategy that led to the Second World War.

Conclusion.

The Occident looks glum, for the rest of the world hates it, but it does not know why. Truth to tell, it does not want to acknowledge that it is no longer a proud Roman emperor who pacified and civilized the world. It is but a fearful obese mummy that wants to remain in power everlastingly. It is a raving lunatic that refuses to educate the young, enrich the poor, and protect the nature that enables it to survive. It is a xenophobic monster whom other monsters want to destroy. As a matter of fact, the failure of the Occident is that of the individual.

The goal of human life is plain and simple: man must become a human being. Hence, he must choose between barbarity and humanity and reason and madness. However, that's not enough, for, in order to challenge his determination, he has to mix with other individuals. In fact, he is bound to become sane and humane within a group of persons whom he helps to become civilized, for no man is an island. Man is not doomed because he lives in a society; he is fortunate to do so, for the best of him comes from disagreement.

For the time being, neither the Occident nor the rest of the world has begotten what I call civilization: societies that enable individuals to become humane, sane humans who perpetuate civilized societies. History of mankind has never existed; what is written in your history books is the history of barbarity. At night, when I close my eyes in order to picture the primeval times, I keep seeing a man setting his hand on a rock face and blowing paint; the trace he leaves behind is the signature of a fearful creature who does not understand he will never own nature, for nature belongs to nature.

It is high time that we broke the curse, for if humanity does not become more reasonable, there will be no better future and no future at all. Man's volition has boundaries. He can choose whomever he wants to become and the kind of society he wants to create, and that's it! He is not allowed to choose between chaos and life, for it was decided once that the perfection of the universe was eternal and unalterable. Human nature, by its very nature, allows man to become perfect and start to create. His wild, twisted thoughts are not allowed to soil the ethereal majesty of the universe.

Nobody but man will save mankind. You can look up and wait for a message from the skies, but they will not speak to you, for they do not want to save you. This heavenly loneliness should lead you to understand that your planet is your destiny. There is no other celestial body in the entire universe that fits your needs. There is no other intelligence in the titanic heights that could help you live your life. Your conscience is your life jacket; your consciousness is your helm. Willpower exists because the highest level of human nature includes intelligence: a state that is not imposed on individuals but freely chosen and which implies that each individual must follow his own path. The consequence of intelligence is the convergence of individual destinies. The greatest minds feel compelled to gather in order to put the finishing touches to this universe invented by someone else. Man is the only creature that is allowed to influence this massive construction. In fact, the gigantic physical masterpiece is awaiting the immaterial oscillation that will reveal the very reason for the existence of everything. No individual alone can do the job, for the element that will unveil the truth is the addition of all the people of good will's willingness to create a better world.

Reasonable people are free, but freedom does not mean that mankind is allowed to do whatever it wants. The choice is not between good and evil, madness and reason, or barbarity and humanity; it is between good and good, reason and reason, and humanity and humanity; it resides in the nuances. Human nature cannot disrupt the celestial mechanism, for Heaven is imploring it to add the finishing touches. The Skies want to rest. So all humans should achieve now the goal which resides in their nature and become creators at last.

Notes.

Part I: The foundations of mediocracy.

Chapter 1: Some mistakes in education.

(1) E. Tony, S. Glantz, "Tobacco industry efforts undermining evidence linking secondhand smoke with cardiovascular disease", *Circulation*, 2007, 116: p. 1845-1854.

(2) L. E. Bero, "Tobacco industry manipulation of research", *Public Health Report*, March-April, 2005, vol. 120, p. 200-208.

(3) C. Velicer, G. St Helen, S. Glantz, "Tobacco papers and tobacco industry ties in *Regulatory toxicology and pharmacology*", February 2018; 39 (1), p.34-48.

(4) T. Legg, M. Legendre, A. Gilmore, "Paying lip service to publication ethics: scientific publishing practices and the Foundation for a Smoke-free World", *Tobacco control*, 2012, p. 65-72.

(5) *World history: patterns of interaction*, McDougal Littell, 2009.

(6) Spielvogel, *Glencoe world history*, 2005, p. 57, 64, 67, 108, 226, 333, **422**, 539.

(7) Rice University, *U. S. history*, Houston, 2021, p. 304, 328, 683.

(8) R. Craknell, R. Tunnicliffe, "Social background of MP's 1971-2019", *Commons Library research briefing*, 15th of February 2022.

(9) "Membership of the 117th Congress: a profile", *Congressional research service*, 14th of December 2022.

(10) *TIMSS 2019 international results in mathematics and science*, Timss and Pirls international study center, 2020. Pisa 2018 results (vol 1): what students know and can do, OECD publishing, 2019. Pisa, *Résultats du PISA 2022 (volume 1); apprentissage et équité dans l'éducation*, 2023, p. 25-26.

(11) "The state of the American student: fall 2022; a guide to pandemic recovery and reinvention", *Center on reinventing public education*, Arizona State University, 2022.

(12) *TIMSS 2019,* p. 18, 38, 159, 171, 175.

(13) *TIMSS 2019,* p. 38, 155, 175. *L'état de l'école 2022,* Direction de l'évaluation, de la prospective et de la performance, 2022, p. 60.

(14) "The state of the American student...", p. 12.

(15) K. S. Cunningham, *Primary education by correspondence,* Melbourne University Press, 1931.

(16) B. Ray, *Research facts on Homeschooling,* National home education research institute, 15th of September 2022.

(17) R. Long, S. Danechi, *Home education in England,* House of Commons library, 19th of December 2022.

Chapter 2: When democracies lie.

(1) Waugh (Paul), "Tony Blair's letters to George Bush", website of the *Huffpost*, 06/07/2016.

(2) "The chair of the Iraqi Inquiry, sir John Chilcot, has spoken exclusively to the BBC's political editor Laura Kuenssberg to mark the first anniversary of the publication of his report into the 2003 invasion. Full transcript of the interview", website of the *BBC*, 6th of July 2017.

(3) G. Evans, J. Mellon, "Immigration, euroscepticism ant the rise and fall of UKIP", *Party Politics*, 2019, vol. 25 (1), p. 76-87.

(4) S. O. Becker, T. Fetzer. D. Novy, "Who voted for Brexit? A comprehensive district-level analysis", *Economic Policy*, October 2017, p. 601-651; **p. 627**.

(5) Evans, p. 79 and 81.

(6) Becker, p. 626-627.

(7)Sarah Lyall, "Johnson's lies worked for years, until they didn't", Website of *The New York Times*, the 8th of July 2022.

(8) A. Blick, P. Hennessy, *Good chaps no more? Safeguarding the constitution in stressful times*, The constitution society, London, 2019.

(9) C. Llewelly, L. Cram, A. Favero, R. L. Hill, "For whom the bell trolls: troll behaviour in the Twitter Brexit debate", Journal of Common Market studies, January 2018.

(10) Glenn Kessler, "Trump made 30 573 false or misleading claims as president. Nearly half came in his final year", website of *The Washington Post*, the 23rd of January 2021.

(11) M. Vazquez, C. Hickey, P. Krishnakumar, J. Boschma, "Donald Trump's presidency by numbers", website of *CNN*, the 18th of December 2020.

(12) Jude Sheerin, "Capitol riots: 'wild' Trump tweet incited attack, says inquiry", website of the *BBC*, the 12th of July 2022.

(13) Tom Dreisbach, "How Trump's 'will be wild!' tweet drew rioters to the Capitol on January 6", website of *The National Public Radio*, the 13th of July 2022.

(14) D. Pion-Berlin, T. Bruneau, R. B. Goetze Jr., "The Trump self-coup attempt: comparisons and civil-military relations", *Government and Opposition*, 2022, p. 1-18.

Chapter 3: The negation of the truth and of the superiority of nature.

(1) World Health Organization, *The world health report 2001; mental health: new understanding, new hope*, Geneva, 2001, p.19 and 23.

(2) World Health Organization, *World mental health report; transforming mental health for all*, Geneva, 2022, p. 37, 39, 45.

(3) Ministry of Health, *Mental health service use in New Zealand 2007/08*, Wellington, 2010, p. VI.

(4) Ministry of Health, *Office of the director of mental health annual report 2016*, Wellington, 2017, p. 4.

(5) La mutualité française, *La santé mentale en France*, Juin 2012, p.5.

(6) S. McManus, P. Bebbigton, R. Jenkins, T. Brugha, *Mental health and well-being in England: adult psychiatric morbidity survey 2014*, Leeds: NHS digital, p. 10.

(7) Australian Bureau of Statistics, *National survey of mental health and well-being: summary of results,* website of the Australian Bureau of Statistics, the 23rd of October 2008.

(8) Australian Bureau of Statistics, *National study of mental health and well-being,* website of the Australian Bureau of Statistics, the 22nd of July 2022.

(9) Mental Health America, *Parity or disparity: the state of mental health in America,* 2015, p. 15 and 18.

(10) Mental Health America, *The state of mental health in America,* 2019, p. 5.

(11) Mental Health America, *The state of mental health in America,* 2022, p. 8.

(12) Laurent Sueur, "Le message médical français concernant les identités de genre (2ème moitié du 19ème siècle-fin du 20ème siècle)", *Déviance et société,* Vol. 20, n° 4, p. 359-375, Liège, 1996.

(13) K. M. Zieselman, "I was an intersex child who had surgery. Don't put other kids through this", website of *USA Today*, undated.

(14) H. Yan, J, Sutton, "Parents sue South Carolina for surgically making child female", website of *CNN*, the 15th of May 2013.

(15) Meredith Bennett-Smith, "Mark and Pam Crawford, parents of intersex child, sue South Carolina for sex assignment surgery", website of *The Huffpost*, the 15th of May 2013.

(16), Olivia Lambert, "M. C. Crawford wins legal battle over intersex surgery", website of *News.com.Au*, the 30th of July 2017.

(17) Laurent Sueur, "Le message médical français...", ibid.

(18) S. Daumas, "Le transsexuel et le psychanaliste", *Corps et langage en psychanalyse*, Lyon, 1980, p. 73-83.

(19) F. Castagnet, "Travestissement, transsexualisme, homosexualité chez l'enfant et l'adolescent", *Traité de psychiatrie de l'enfant et de l'adolescent,* Paris, 1985, p. 663-680.

(20) L. Erickson-Schroth, *Trans bodies, trans selves, a resource for the transgender community,* Oxford University Press, New York, 2014.

(21) Ministerio de Sanidad, *Encuesta nacional de salud España 2017*, Madrid, 2018.

(22) Australian Bureau of Statistics, *Overweight and obesity (2017-2018)*, website of the Australian Bureau of Statistics, the 12th of December 2018. J. Dawson, R. Morland, R. Brooks, *A picture of overweight and obesity in Australia (2017)*, Australian Institute of Health and Welfare, Canberra, 2017.

(23) Ministry of Health of New Zealand, *Obesity in 2021/22: an experimental analysis using data from general practices*, Wellington, 2022, p. 4.

(24) C. Fryar, M. Carroll, C. Ogden, *Prevalence of overweight, obesity, and severe obesity among adults aged 20 and over: United States, 1960-1962 through 2015-2016,* National Center for Health Statistics, 2018, p. 1 and 3.

(25) C. Fryar, M. Carroll, C. Ogden, *Prevalence of overweight, obesity, and severe obesity among children and adolescents aged 2-19 years: United States, 1963-1965 through 2015-2016,* National Center for Health Statistics, 2018, p. 1 and 3.

(26) Drew Desilver, "What's on your table? How America's diet has changed over the decades", website of *Pew Research Center*, the 13th of December 2016.

Part II: Man as the enemy of man.

Chapter 4: When freedom leads to murder and imprisonment.

(1) US Fish and Wildlife Service, "Annual hunting and fishing license sales", various dates, website of the *US Fish and Wildlife Service.*

(2) National Shooting Sports Foundation, *Target shooting in America, an economic force for conservation*, 2018, p. 2.

(3) Smith (Tom W.), Son (Jaesok), "Trends in gun ownership in the United States, 1972-2014", *General social survey, final report*, March 2015, p. 5.

(4)Ted Van Green, "Wide differences on most gun policies between gun owners and non-owners, but also some agreement", website of *Pew Research Center*.

(5) Educational Fund to Stop Gun Violence and Coalition to Stop Gun Violence, *A public health crisis decades in the making: a review of 2019 CDC gun mortality data*, 2021, p. 4.

(6) "Gun violence statistics for the year 2022", website of *Gun Violence Archive,* the 25th of March 2023.

(7) ... *A public health crisis...*, p.14.

(8) Laurent Sueur, *The pathological manifestations of contemporary societies: a psychological study on immaturity and its social implications, with color illustrations*, chapter 9, the American psychopaths, p. 178-203, 2023.

(9) *The pathological manifestations...*, p. 181. The mirror phase in explained on page 180.

(10) *The pathological manifestations...*, p. 193.

(11) *The pathological manifestations...*, p. 194.

(12) *The pathological manifestations...*, p. 195.

(13) *The pathological manifestations...*, p. 192.

(14) *The pathological manifestations...*, p. 194.

(15) *The pathological manifestations...*, p. 194.

(16) W. Sawyer and P. Wagner, "Mass incarceration: the whole pie 2022", *Prison Policy Initiative*, 2022, p. 21.

(17) Mass incarceration..., p. 22.

(18) Mass incarceration..., p. 2.

(19) Mass incarceration..., p. 26.

(20) Mass incarceration..., p. 12.

(21) Mass incarceration..., p. 16.

(22) H. Fair and R. Walmsley, *World prison population list*, 2012, p.6-14.

(23) H. Fair..., p. 7. I have added the incarcerated Uyghurs and the persons who await trial in jail.

(24) Mass incarceration..., p. 24.

(25) Mass incarceration..., p. 28.

(26) Max Fisher, "Other countries had mass murders. Then they changed their gun laws", website of *The New York Times*, the 25th of May 2022.

(27) Council of Australian Governments, *National firearms agreement*, February 2017, p. 2 and 3.

(28) Zack Beauchamps, "Australia confiscated 650 000 guns. Murders and suicides plummeted", website of *Vox*, the 25th of May 2022.

(29) "Gun ownership figures revealed 25 years on from the Port Arthur massacre", website of the *University of Sydney*, the 28th of April 2021.

(30) R. Ramchand and J. Saunders, "The effects of the 1996 National Firearms Agreement in Australia on suicide, homicide, and mass shooting", *Contemporary issues in gun policy*, website of *RAND Corporation*, the 15th of April 2021.

(31) "Homicide in Australia from 1989 to 2020", website of *The Australian Institute of Criminology*, tables 1, 2, 15 and 16. "Rate of gun homicides in Australia from 1988 to 2018", website of *Australian gun safety alliance.*

(32) "Suicide deaths by sex in Australia from 1991 to 2021", website of *The Australian Institute of Health and Welfare.*

Chapter 5: Perpetual racism.

(1) Laurent Sueur, *The pathological manifestations of contemporary societies: a psychological study on immaturity and its social implications, with color illustrations*, 2023, p. 135 and 136.

(2) Josephine Baker, "Speech delivered on the 28th of August 1963 at the March on Washington", Website of *Blackpas*t, the 3rd of November 2011.

(3) *The pathological manifestations...*, p. 136-139.

(4) US Department of Justice, Federal Bureau of Investigation, *Hate crime statistics*, 1996, 1997, 1998, 1999, 2000, 2001, 2002, 2003-2009, 2010-2019. FBI National Press Office, *FBI releases supplemental 2021 hate crime statistics*, the 13th of March 2023.

(5)Australian hate crime network, *Community profiles of hate crime and hate incidents in Australia,* 2022, p. 10.

(6) Reconciliation Australia, *Australian Reconciliation Barometer*, 2022, p. 5.

(7) A. Thurber et al., "Prevalence of everyday discrimination and relation with well-being among Aboriginal and Torres Strait Islander adults in Australia", *International Journal of Environmental Research and Public Health*, 2021, 18, 6577.

(8) Australian hate crime network, *Community profiles of hate crime and hate incidents in Australia,* 2022, p. 15.

(9) Laurent Sueur, *The pathological manifestations...*, p. 215, 216.

(10) Laurent Sueur, *The pathological manifestations...*, p. 220-222.

(11) Laurent Sueur, *The pathological manifestations...*, p. 170-174.

(12) CNCDH, *La lutte contre le racisme, l'antisémitisme et la xénophobie, année 2022,* Paris, 2023, p. 33.

(13) CNCDH, *La lutte contre le racisme...*, p. 177-178, notes 74 and 75.

(14) Laurent Sueur, *The pathological manifestations...*, p. 143-151. The picture comes from: https://www.liberation.fr/resizer/BbcBt5xlt2w8FuCmSPI7K4F4iYM=/600x0/filters:format(jpg):quality(70):focal(4774x3898:4784x3908)/cloudfront-eu-c liberation/TPVYSMPIBRGEFFZROBTRUJDIPQ.jpg.

(15) Laurent Sueur, *The pathological manifestations...*, p. 147-148.

(16) E. Ball, M. Steffens, C. Niedlich, "Racism in Europe: characteristics and intersections with other social categories", *Frontiers in Psychology*, vol. 13, March 2022, p. 7.

(17) E. Ball, "Racism in Europe..., p. 8.

(18) E. Ball, "Racism in Europe..., p. 9.

(19) CNCDH, *La lutte contre le racisme, l'antisémitisme et la xénophobie, 2014* (p. 37), *2015* (p. 31), *2016* (p. 53), *2022* (p. 129).

(20) Alina Rzepnikowska, "Racism and xenophobia experienced by Polish migrants in the UK before and after Brexit vote", *Journal of Ethnic and Migration Studies*, 2019, vol. 45, n° 1, p. 62 and 70.

(21) Michael Mutch, "Arkadiusz Jozwik manslaughter in Harlow: the full sentencing remarks", website of *EssexLive*, the 8th of September 2017.

(22) CNCDH, *La lutte contre le racisme, l'antisémitisme et la xénophobie, année 2014,* Paris, 2015, p. 32.

(23) CNCDH, *La lutte contre le racisme, l'antisémitisme et la xénophobie, année 2022,* Paris, 2023, p. 129, 135, 136.

Chapter 6: The conflict between genders and that between generations.

(1) Laurent Sueur, *The pathological manifestations of contemporary societies: a psychological study on immaturity and its social implications, with color illustrations*, 2023, p. 143-151.

(2) "Écart de rémunération entre hommes et femmes en Europe: faits et chiffres", website of *The European Parliament*, the 4th of March 2020.

(3) Kochhar (Rakesh), "The enduring grip of the gender pay gap", website of *Pew Research Center*, the 1st of March 2023.

(4) "Monthly ranking of women in national parliaments", website of *Inter-parliamentary Union*, the 1st of July 2023.

(5) "Women in elective office 2023", website of *Center for American women and politics.*

(6) National Coalition Against Domestic Violence, "Domestic violence", website of *NCADV*.

(7) "Family, domestic and sexual violence", website of the *Australian Institute of Health and Welfare*, the 3rd of February 2023.

(8) European Union Agency for fundamental rights, *Violence à l'égard des femmes: une enquête à l'échelle de l'UE,* Luxembourg, 2014.

(9) Insituto Nacional de Estadística, "Total nacional de la violencia de género"; "Notas de prensas", the 31st of May 2023.

(10) Official statistics of Sweden, *Swedish Crime Survey 2022*, p. 12 and 16.

(11) Khoshnood (A.), Ohlsson (H.), Sundquist (J.), Sundquist (K.), "Swedish rape offenders – a latent class analysis", *Forensic Science Research*, 2021, Vol. 6, n° 2, p. 124-132.

(12) Wemrell (M.), Stjernlöf (S.), Lila (M.), Gracia (E.), Ivert (A.-K.), "The Nordic Paradox. Professionals' s discussions about gender

equality and intimate partner violence against women in Sweden", *Women and Criminal Justice*, volume 32, 2022, issue 5, p. 431-453.

(13) Francioli (S. P.), Danbold (F.), North (M. S.), "Millennials versus Boomers: an asymmetric pattern of realistic and symbolic threats drives intergenerational tensions in the United States", *Personality and Social Psychology Bulletin*, the 3rd of May 2023.

(14) Harris (John), "The gap between young and old has turned Britain into a dysfunctional family", website of *The Guardian*, the 12th of January 2020.

(15) "La pauvreté augmente chez les plus jeunes, mais aussi chez les 50-64 ans", website of the *Centre d'observation de la société*, the 20th of September 2020.

(16) Fondation Jean Jaurès, *Générations: le grand fossé*, 2022.

(17) Inspection générale de la Justice and Inspection générale de l'administration, Mission d'analyse des profils des délinquants interpellés à l'occasion de l'épisode de violence urbaines (27 juin-7 juillet): rapport définitif, 2023, p. 23-33.

(18) Romain Gueugneau and Édouard Lederer, "Emeutes: près de 400 agences bancaires vandalisées", website of *Les Échos*, the 5th of July 2023.

Part III: Economic issues.

Chapter 7: Mass unemployment and poverty in the Occident.

(1) European Anti-Poverty Network, *Poverty Report Sweden 2019*, October 2019, p. 3.

(2) *Poverty Report Sweden...*, p. 5.

(3) Alm (S.), Nelson (K.), Nieuwenhuis (R.), "The diminishing power of one? Welfare state retrenchment and rising poverty of single-adult households in Sweden 1988-2011", *European sociological review*, 2020, vol. 36, n° 2, p. 204.

(4) European Social Policy Network, *In-work poverty in Sweden*, 2019, p. 4, 5, 7, 8.

(5) *Poverty Report Sweden...*, p. 6.

(6) Henley (J.), "Sweden has a poverty problem: the social stores offering food at rock-bottom prices", website of *The Guardian*, the 5th of December 2022.

(7) Nicolas Baverez, "La spécificité française du chômage structurel de masse, des années 1930 aux années 1990", *Vingtième siècle,* n° 52, October-December 1996, p. 41-65.

(8) Observatoire des inégalités, *Rapport sur la pauvreté en France, 2ème édition: 2020-2021*, 2020.

(9) Observatoire des inégalités..., p. 25.

(10) Observatoire des inégalités..., p. 86 and 87.

(11) Secours catholique, *État de la pauvreté en France 2022; à l'épreuve des crises: enquête sur les budgets des plus précaires,* November 2022, p. 4.

(12) Ministère de la santé et de la prévention, Direction de la recherche, des études, de l'évaluation et des statistiques, *Minima sociaux*

et prestations sociales, fiche 1: "Les caractéristiques des personnes pauvres et des personnes modestes", p.24.

(13) Observatoire des inégalités..., p. 77.

(14) Observatoire des inégalités..., p. 61.

(15) Observatoire des inégalités..., p. 94.

(16) Antonio Argandoña, *Una historia del desempleo en España,* 1999, p. 66.

(17) Departamento de Análisis de Bankinter, "Cifras del paro: el número de parados aumento en octubre en + 36 936 personas", website of *Bankinter*, the 3rd of November 2023.

(18) European Anti-Poverty Network, *El estado de la pobreza en las comunidades autónomas*, May 2023, p. 26.

(19) *El estado de la pobreza...,* p. 30.

(20) *El estado de la pobreza...,* p. 32.

(21) US Bureau of Labor Statistics, retrieved from FRED, Federal Reserve Bank of St. Louis; https://fred.stlouisfed.org/series/UNRATE, December 24, 2023.

(22) Shrider (E. A.), Creamer (J.), *Poverty in the United States: 2022; current population report,* United States Census Bureau, September 2023, p. 3.

(23)Matthew Desmond, "Why poverty persists in America: a Pulitzer prize-winning sociologist offers a new explanation for an intractable problem", website of *The New York Times*, the 9th of March 2023.

(24) Oxfam America, *The crisis of low wages in the US; who makes less than $ 15 an hour in 2022?,* 2022, p. 3 and 8.

(25) Matthew Desmond...

(26) US Bureau of Labor Statistics, *A profile of the working poor, 2022,* report 1099, website of the *US Bureau of Labor Statistics*, September 2022.

(27) Jeremy Ney, "The surprising poverty lands across the US", website of *Time Magazine,* the 4th of October 2023.

(28) "BLS now publishing Monthly Data for American Indians and Alaska Natives", website of the *US Bureau of Labor Statistics*, the 14th of February 2022.

(29) US Bureau of Labor Statistics, "Comparing unemployment rates by race: the Great Recession versus COVID-19", website of the *Federal Reserve Bank of St. Louis*, the 23rd of May 2022.

(30) Oxfam America..., p. 11.

(31) Jeremy Ney...

(32) US Bureau of Labor Statistics, "Unemployment rate-Black or African Americans", website of the *Federal Reserve Bank of St. Louis*, the 3rd of November 2023.

(33) Oxfam America..., p. 8, 11, 13, and 16.

Chapter 8: Overconsumption and the pillage of resources.

(1) Rosenberg (E. S.), "Le 'modèle américain' de la consommation de masse", *Cahiers d'histoire; Revue d'histoire critique*, n° 108, 2009, p. 111-142.

(2) WWF and Global Footprint Network, *Jour du dépassement de la terre 2022, nos systèmes agricoles et alimentaires en question*, 2022, p, 2, 5, 6, 7, and 8.

(3) Lakshmi (R. B.), "The environmental impact of battery production for electric vehicles", website of *Earth.org*, the 11th of January 2023.

(4) Zheng (M.), "The environmental impact of lithium and cobalt mining", website of *Earth.org*, the 31st of March 2023.

(5) National Commission on the BP Deepwater Horizon oil spill and offshore drilling, *Deep water: the gulf oil disaster and the future of offshore drilling*, January 2011.

(6) National Commission on the BP Deepwater Horizon oil spill..., p. 30.

(7) National Commission on the BP Deepwater Horizon oil spill..., p. 34.

(8) National Commission on the BP Deepwater Horizon oil spill..., p. 41.

(9) National Commission on the BP Deepwater Horizon oil spill..., p. 50.

(10) Republic of the Marshal Island, office of the Maritime Administrator, *Deepwater Horizon marine casualty investigation report*, 2011.

(11) National Commission on the BP Deepwater Horizon oil spill..., p. 169.

(12) National Commission on the BP Deepwater Horizon oil spill..., p. 167.

(13) National Commission on the BP Deepwater Horizon oil spill..., p. 122; Republic of the Marshal Island..., p. 49.

(14) Allison (E.), Mandler (B.), *Petroleum and the environment,* American geosciences institute, 2018, part 7.

(15) Buonocore (J. J.) et al., "Air pollution and health impacts of oil and gas production in the United States", *Environmental Research: Health,* 1, 2023, 021006.

(16) Marappan (R.) et al., *Assessment of the impacts of the offshore oil and gas industry on the marine environment,* OSPAR's Quality Status Report 2023, p. 37.

(17) Marappan (R.) et al..., p. 34.

(18) Weng (Z.) et al., "Pollutant loads from coal mining in Australia: discerning trends from the National Pollutant Inventory", *Environmental Science and Policy*, 19-20, 2012, p. 78-89.

(19) Ryan (B.), et al., *Radionuclides and metals in freshwater mussels of the upper South Alligator River,* internal report 487, February 2005, Australian Government: Department of the Environment and Heritage Supervising Scientist.

Chapter 9: Westerners confronted with climate change.

(1) European Investment Bank, *The EIB climate survey 2019-2020; how citizens are confronting the climate crisis and what actions they expect from policymakers and businesses*, 2020, p. 9.

(2) Bentolila (S.), Borstein (R.), Calatayud (B.), "Climatoscepticisme: le nouvel horizon du populisme français", website of *Fondation Jean Jaurès*, the 26th of April 2023.

(3) *The EIB climate survey...*, p. 30, 31, 32, 33, 43 and 54.

(4) White (R. H.) et al., "The unprecedented Pacific Northwest heatwave of June 2021", *Nature Communications*, 2023, 14:727.

(5) White (R. H.)..., p. 6 and 7.

(6) White (R. H.)..., p. 9.

(7) Andreadis (K. M.) and Lettenmaier (D. P.), "Trends in 20th century drought over the continental United States", *Geographical research letter*, vol. 33, L 10403, 2006.

(8) Copernicus, "L' été 2022 est le plus chaud jamais enregistré en Europe", website of *Copernicus*, Bonn, the 8th of September 2022.

(9) Ministerio para la transición ecológica y el reto demógrafico, *Impactos y riesgos derivados del cambio climático en España,* 2021, p. 55.

(10) Real instituto elcano, Los españoles ante el cambio climático; Apoyo ciudadano a los elementos, instrumentos y procesos de una Ley de Cambio Climático y Transición Energética, 2019, p. 15.

(11) Jose Luis Escudero Gallegos, "¿Veremos algunas vez el Embalse de la Viñuela al 98%? Fotos de una primavera 2011 esplendorosa", website of *Diario Sur*, the 26th of September 2021. Tejada (Paula), "El Gobierno aprueba la construcción de una desaladora en Málaga para hacer frente a la sequía", website of *Málaga Hoy*, the 11th of May 2023.

(12) Martín Morales (I.), "El embalse de la Viñuela agoniza a la espera de un otoño lluvioso", website of *Málagahoy*, the 11th of September 2023.

(13) Pedrosa (J.), "Málaga toma la primera gran medida contra la sequía y reduce le pressión del agua", website of *Málagahoy*, the 19th of January 2024.

(14) Ramos (María), "Los agricultores de la Axarquía se ven obligados a arrancar sus plantaciones debido a la falta de agua", website of *Málagahoy*, the 1st of August 2022.

(15) AEOPAS, *Informe de situación de la sequía en Andalucía*, 2024.

(16) Redacción de Málagahoy, "El uso de las desaladoras en Málaga contra la sequía", website of *Málagahoy*, the 23rd of January 2024.

(17) Tejada (Paula), "El gobierno aprueba la construcción de una desaladora en Málaga para hacer frente a la sequía", website of *Málagahoy*, the 11th of May 2023.

Part IV: A besieged fortress.

Chapter 10: Immigration.

(1) Saad (Lydia), "Americans still value immibration, but have concerns", website of *Gallup*, the 13th of July 2023; editorial staff of Gallup, "Immigration", website of *Gallup*, 2023.

(2) Budiman (Abby), "Key findings about US immigrants", website of *Pew Research Center*, the 20th of August 2020.

(3) Passel (J. S.), Krogstadt (J. M.), "What we know about unauthorized immigrants living in the US", website of *Pew Research Center*, the 16th of November 2023.

(4) Law (Robert), "FY2023: the worst year on record for illegal immigration", website of *America First Policy Institute*, the first of November 2023.

(5) Garsd (Jasmine), "An unprecedented year in immigration and anti-immigration rhetoric", website of *NPR*, the 22nd of December 2023.

(6) Editorial staff of PBS, "The road to the General Election", website of *PBS*, the 7th of February 2024; the figures come from the Marist Institute for Public Opinion.

(7) Garsd, "An unprecedented...

(8) Santhanam (Laura), "Where voters stand on immigration", website of *PBS*, the 7th of February 2024.

(9) Rose (Joel), "Despite efforts of 3 US administrations, migrant families keep crossing the border", website of *NPR*, the 23rd of September 2023.

(10) Dumont (Gérard-François), "L'immigration en Europe: quelle évolution démographique, quelles dynamiques gégraphiques,

quels facteurs géopolitiques?", *Les analyse de population et avenir*, 2019/1, n° 5, p. 4.

(11) "Significant rise in irregular border crossings in 2023, biggest since 2016", website of *Frontex*, the 26th of January 2024.

(12) Editorial staff of the Middle East Monitor, "41 migrants believed dead in shipwreck off Italy", website of the *Middle East Monitor*, the 9th of August 2023.

(13) Commission européenne, "Statistiques sur la migration vers l' Europe", website of the *Commission européenne*, undated.

Chapter 11: Islamic terrorism.

(1) Usamah Bin Muhammad Bin Ladin, "Declaration of Jihad Against the Americans Occupying the Land of the Two Holiest Sites", website of *Masarykova univerzita*, https://is.muni.cz/el/1423/jaro2010/MVZ203/OBL___AQ__Fatwa_1996.pdf.

(2) "Al Qaeda's Second Fatwa", website of *PBS*, the 23rd of February 1998.

(3) "Bin Laden's letter to America", website of *The Guardian*, the 24th of November 2002.

(4) United States foreign broadcast information service report, Compilation of Osama Bin Laden statements: 1994-January 2004, p. 82.

(5) Op. cit., p. 4.

(6) Op. cit., p. 11.

(7) Op. cit., p.16.

(8) Op. cit., p. 17.

(9) Op. cit., p. 27.

(10) Op. cit., p. 31.

(11) Op. cit., p. 33.

(12) Op. cit., p. 34.

(13) Op. cit., p. 99.

(14) Op. cit., p. 221.

(15) Pennebaker, James, Chung, Cindy, "computerized text analysis of Al Qaeda transcripts", in Krippendorf, Klaus, Bock, Mary-Angela, *The content analysis reader*, Thousand oak, 2009.

(16) United States foreign broadcast information service report, *Compilation of Osama Bin Laden statements: 1994-January 2004*, p. 140.

(17) Op. cit., p. 79.

(18) Op. cit., p. 86.

(19) Op. cit., p. 82.

(20) Op. cit., p. 86.

(21) Op. Cit., p. 11.

(22) Op. cit., p. 120.

(23) Op. cit., p. 14.

(24) Op. cit., p. 147.

(25) Lankford, Adam, "A psychological autopsy of 9/11 ringleader Mohamed Atta", *Journal of police and criminal psychology*, 2012, vol. 27, p. 150-159.

(26) Atta, Mohamed, "Im Namen Gottes, des Allmächtigen", *Der Spiegel*, the 1st of October 2001. English translation by Imad Musa (Capital communications group).

(27) Ibid.

(28) Ibid.

(29) Campelo (Nicolas) et ali., "Who are the European youths willing to engage in radicalization? A multidisciplinary review of their psychological and social profiles", *European Psychiatry*, 52, 2018, p. 1-14.

(30) Campelo (Nicolas) et ali., "Joining the Islamic State from France between 2014 and 2016: an observational follow-up study", *Palgrave Communications*, 2018, 4, 137.

(31) Loch, Dietmar, "Moi, Khaled Kelkal", *Le monde*, the 7th of October 1995, p. 10. In 1992, Dietmar Loch, who was writing his thesis, interviewed Khaled Kelkal.

(32) The word is used in English, but it is a French idea. Since the French are obliged to speak the language spoken by the French civil servants, all the regional dialects are regarded as slang nowadays.

(33) Ibid.

(34) Penin, Alain, *Expertise psychologique de Mohamed Merah*, tribunal correctionnel, 3ème chambre, Toulouse, 2009.

(35) A neurotic personality is always stable.

(36) Doria, Jean-Charles, *Mohamed Merah, itinéraire d'un tueur*, Kalisté productions-France Télévision, movie, France, 2013.

(37) Lebourg (E.), "L'enfance miserable des frères Kouachi", website of *Reporterre*, the 15th of January 2015.

(38) Faure (S.), Tourencheau (P.) and Le Devin (W.), "Amédy Coulibaly, une personnalité immature et psychopatique", website of *Libération*, the 9th of January 2015.

(39) Harounyan (S.) et ali., "Sur les traces du tueur de Nice", website of *Libération*, the 17th of July 2016. "Attack on Nice: who was Mohamed Lahouaiej-Bouhlel?", website of the BBC, the 19th of August 2016. Renac (G.), "Mohamed Lahouaiej-Bouhlel: une proie facile à recruiter", website of *Le Journal du Dimanche*, the 18th of July 2016.

(40) Chevalier (J.), "Il avait deux personnalités: les parents du terroriste de Nice se posent toujours la question du 'pourquoi'", website of *BFMTV*, the 26th of October 2022.

Chapter 12: Nationalism.

(1) Doving (Cora Alexa), "Muslims Are..." in *The Shifting Boundaries of Prejudice. Antisemitism and Islamophobia in Contemporary Norway*, Scandinavian University Press, 2020, p. 254-273.

(2) Eriksen (T. H.), *Immigration and national identity in Norway*, Migration Policy Institute, 2013.

(3) Hervik (Peter), "Denmark's blond vision and the fractal logics of a nation in danger", *Identities: global studies in culture and power*, 2019.

(4) Tomson (D. L.), "The rise of Sweden Democrats: Islam, Populism and the end of the Swedish exceptionalism", website of *Brookings*, the 25th of March 2020.

(5) Belin (C.) and Dollar (D.), "What's driving populism's rise on both sides of the Atlantic?", website of *Brookings*, the 21st of January 2020.

(6) Tomson (D. L.), "The rise of Sweden Democrats...

(7) https://www.levif.be/international/europe/espagne-vox-le-parti-dextreme-droite-qui-espere-creer-la-surprise/.

(8) Mayor Ortega (Leonor), "Vox quiere privilegiar la inmigración procedente de América Latina", website of *Lavanguardia*, the 20th of Mars 2019.

(9) Cembrero (Ignacio), "Vox y la inmigración: un programa electoral radical de imposible cumplimiento", website of Elconfidencial, the 8th of July 2023.

(10) Fuentes (Isabel), "Vow propone que las fuerzas armadas combaten la inmigración ilegal porque cree que tiene vínculo con el terrorismo", website of *20minutos,* the 11th of October 2023. Fuentes (Isabel), "Vow ordena a sus dirigentes autonómicos rechazar el reparto

de inmigrantes y asume que su postura generara tensión con el PP", website of *20minutos*, the 31st of October 2023.

(11) Winfield (Nicole), "How a party of neo-fascist roots won big in Italy", website of *Apnews*, the 26th of September 2023.

(12) https://upload.wikimedia.org/wikipedia/commons/thumb/b/b6/Giorgia_Meloni_Official_2023_crop.jpg/800px-Giorgia_Meloni_Official_2023_crop.jpg

www.ingramcontent.com/pod-product-compliance
Lightning Source LLC
LaVergne TN
LVHW050549160826
845677LV00011B/2237

* 9 7 9 8 2 2 4 0 7 8 3 1 8 *